SERENDIPITY QUILTS

by Sara Nephew

MIRRORS FOR REPEATS

Two mirrors taped together with a thread across the top limiting them to a 60° angle allows a preview of what designs might result from a particular fabric. Just place the taped mirrors at the top of the Super 60™ and tape the thread. The designs are not exact, since this shows a repeat and its reverse three times, instead of six repeats, but it gives a good idea of the look you will get.

OUTLINE

SPECIAL THANKS

The author owes a debt of gratitude to the talented quilters who are willing to try an untested pattern. They may set the standard for the quilt, they sometimes find errors and correct them, they make changes and suggestions. They also come up with new ideas for layouts and corner treatments. This time sincere thanks are due to: Virginia Anderson, Annette Austin, Laurie Bevan, Juanita Canfield, Diane Coombs, Pam Cope, Stephanie Davis, Joan Dawson, Joanne File, Bill Flynn, Linda Gentry, Janet Goad, Eda Lee Haas, Joan Hansen, Scott Hansen, Judy Irish, Nadi Lane, Kathie Kryla, Kathleen Malarky, Pearl Mok, Suzanne Nelson, Vickie Nysether, Sally Parker, Pam Pifer, Carole Rush, Terri Shinn, Kathleen Springer, and George Taylor. Thanks also to the small group called "Loose Threads" for making above and beyond contributions as pattern testers. To all of you, thanks for creating beautiful quilts!

DEDICATION

To the Monday Night Bowlers, my bi-weekly small group. We have been together for 19 years, with few changes. Now what can we be but friends! We provide encouragement, both professional and personal, for all our members. They told me to do this book. (As a satellite group to Seattle's Quilters Anonymous, they decided to remain anonymous. Hence the name. A couple of the members had small children who thought they were actually going bowling every other Monday. This was years ago.)

CREDITS

Photography by Terry Reed
Cover Graphics by Elizabeth Nephew

SERENDIPITY QUILTS

Clearview Triangle
8311 180th St. S.E.
Snohomish, WA 98296-4802

Library of Congress Control Number: 2002096389
ISBN 1-930294-04-2

SERENDIPITY QUILTS

INTRODUCTION

"Serendipity" can be defined as "happy accident". An accident of timing, many things coming together just right, created all these quilt designs. And this kind of quilt capitalizes on beautiful designs created by repeat fabric patterns coming together (almost accidentally) like a kaleidoscope. So "Serendipity Quilts" seemed like a proper title.

In the 1970's, as I began quilting, the natural thing was to try many different techniques and types of quilts. One that definitely caught my interest was the Grandmother's Flower Garden pattern, made with English Paper Piecing. One of the fun things a quilter could do using these techniques was to choose an element of a fabric print (a flower for example), center it in a hexagon, and repeat it all around the block. Beautiful blocks were created this way. I made several blocks and one and a half pincushions.

But it was so slow! Too much time went into making one design, when so many beautiful quilts were out there, waiting to be discovered. So I gave up English Paper Piecing and moved on to rotary cutting and speed-pieced quilts.

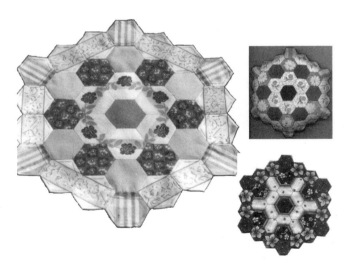

But I was still entranced by 60° shapes, and by carefully placed fabric designs. By 2002 I had written seven quilt books with patterns based on rotary cut 60° triangles, diamonds, etc. Now new methods of creating repeated pattern motifs have been developed. We can stack six identical sections of the same fabric, then cut them all at once to create sets of repeats. Wow! Let's put stacked repeats into 60° quilt designs!

CHOOSING REPEAT FABRICS

After making one of these quilts, you may find yourself always keeping an eye out for good repeat fabrics for a Serendipity quilt. What is needed is six repeats of a **high contrast large print**. I like a fabric with motifs floating on either a light or dark background. Some space between these motifs is desirable. Or other designs may be edge to edge, but in different colors, dividing motifs that way. Many variations are possible. Of course, quilting requires a blouse weight 100% cotton fabric.

Some fabrics have tight designs that are limited in space, and then repeated over and over. These fabrics may have a short repeat like 12-13 inches, and so you will only need to purchase about 2¼ - 2½ yards. This may provide enough layered repeats for a whole quilt. Cinco de Mayo, pg. 49, was pieced with a short repeat like this. Another large print high contrast fabric may be a big swishy floral (looking like watercolor brush strokes) with a long repeat, and you may need to buy four yards or more. Or a unique print may require more waste to create attractive designs, so you might want to buy double the repeats just to make sure you have enough fabric to work with.

When you get your beautiful fabric home, you can choose a block design from this book that is most likely to fit the scale of the motifs on the fabric.

Leftover Repeat Fabrics

If you have chosen a high contrast large print fabric that has a big repeat, there may be a whole panel left over, or even more. Are you going to end up with a closet full of leftovers of large prints? But there are ways to use these scraps.

Someone in your guild might appreciate being able to buy a prewashed length of fabric for their own Serendipity Quilt. Or you could incorporate the panel into the back of the quilt. In fact, it would be a good idea to put part of the repeat fabric into the quilt back anyway. People are constantly surprised by what the repeats produced, and it's fun to show the original fabric.

> **To learn more about stacked pattern repeats**, read Bethany Reynolds' books, "Magic Stack 'N Whack Quilts®", "Stack 'N Whackier," and "Magic Quilts-By The Slice ."

STACKED REPEATS - PREPARING A STACK

1. **Buy six repeats (plus) of a high-contrast large print.** Wash, dry, and press selvage to selvage. (Buy a little extra to make it easier to choose the memory point.)

2. **Make a notch at the fold and tear fabric in half lengthwise**. This gives you two easy to handle lengths of six design repeats each. Set one length aside.

3. On the remaining length, along the selvage or the inside torn edge, near one cut end, **find a memory point (a particular detail, like a leaf or seashell) that will make it easy to see the six repeats.** Find the next occurrence of this detail along the same long edge, being sure there is one whole repeat between this and the previous occurrence. At this memory point, lay a 6" x 24" clear ruler across the width of the fabric section. Find more reference points across the width of the fabric, lining the ruler up perpendicular to the selvage edge. Keeping these reference points in mind and finding them again each time, cut six repeats apart with a rotary cutter, making six identical panels from the original length of fabric.

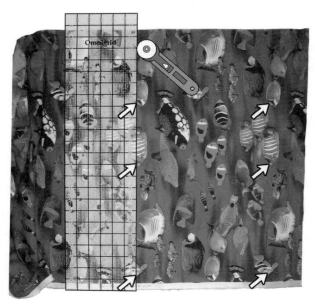

The arrows point up details showing where the printed fish pattern begins to repeat itself. Notice at the right edge where having a few extra inches of fabric allows you to choose where you want to cut the repeats.

4. **Place the repeat sections on top of each other. Count the layers to make sure you have six repeats. Find a design detail again, a precise point (like the tip of a line) that is easy to see, and place a pin in it.** Work from the top down, resting your hand on the stacked layers of fabric. Put the pin point in the detail, then pull the first layer up onto the pin, placing the excess over your hand holding the pin. Repeat with the next layer, keeping the pin in the same position, only moving slightly as necessary to precisely pierce the same detail. When a detail is pierced through all layers, pin the layers together using a tight small stitch not bigger than ¼". Do this over the whole stack, using a pin every 4-6 inches in all directions. If you have a large repeat, you might have to start in the center and work out, otherwise you can work from one end to the other. During this process, you may shake and smooth the whole stack when necessary to make the layers lay flat. When the stack is pinned overall, touch with an iron here and there to mesh some fibers on the layers.

5. **Trim one cut edge of the stacked panels removing pins as necessary. Then cut** a 3½" (or according to the block pattern requirement) strip thru all the panels for triangles, or a 3¼" (or according to the block pattern requirement) strip for diamonds and flat pyramids. Again, remove the pins in that area first, so the ruler lays flat, and to be sure there isn't a pin in front of your rotary cutter. You may wish to waste some background fabric when cutting the strips to obtain the most beautiful design repeats.

6. **Cut diamonds or triangles from the layered strip.** (See cutting directions on pgs 7-13.) Position the diamond or triangle to get the most attractive motif on the shape, again wasting a little fabric if necessary.

Try Stacking With Thread

The arrow shows the leaf tip, a good precise detail to choose for stacking

Using a needle and thread: The arrow shows the needle (with a knotted thread) being inserted at the leaf tip. Then fold the top fabric up over your hand holding the needle, so you can see to insert it at the same place in the next fabric panel. When all six panels are on the needle and the needle is straight up and down through all the layers, take a small tight stitch, and then a few backstitches to anchor the stitch.

HELPFUL HINTS

As you work on Serendipity Quilts, you will learn more about choosing and using patterned fabric, buying repeats, making decisions in the middle of a project, etc. Here are some comments about methods that may produce even more gorgeous quilts. Thanks to Joan Dawson and Virginia Anderson for some of these suggestions.

1. Be sure - buy enough fabric to get six repeats. Numerous times helpful quilt shop workers, fabric manufacturers, etc., or myself, have done quick math and estimated yardage, only to have me find (at home, when beginning a project) that I only have four or maybe five repeats. You can find part of the repeat on the other lengthwise half of your fabric piece, but this will make the rest of the other half unusable for repeats, although perhaps it will have some other use. (On the back of the quilt, maybe.) So not buying enough fabric to start with is actually wasteful of fabric. To be sure, stand in the store and count the repeats using a motif or pattern detail along the selvage edge. Then get extra to give yourself a choice of where to begin cutting the repeat sections apart.

2. Be sure - buy enough fabric(s) to make a beautiful quilt. (This may require some thought, see #3 below.) Generally you will need a variety of fabrics to make a colorful, well-balanced design. If you are an experienced quilter, you have a collection to work from, but even then you may not have stocked up on large prints that cut up well, or motifs that are great for fussy cutting. Be sure you have a yard or two of each supporting fabric you are considering for the quilt. If the second half of your repeat fabric is left over, or if you end up not using a two-yard piece of accent fabric, maybe it'll be just perfect on the back, or for a future quilt. It doesn't matter as much if you are willing to jump up from your sewing and go buy another piece of fabric, but that's often not convenient. As you are making blocks and setting triangles, be willing to try new fabrics to refresh the color scheme or balance the weight of a pattern.

3. Take time to think a bit about your fabric. I took this hint from Virginia, and laid my main fabric out on the floor recently after I had already begun to cut repeats in half of it. While watching television, I glanced at the material, appreciating and getting to know the shapes and designs scattered across the weave. Then I realized that I had begun cutting repeats in such a way that I was basically eliminating one of my favorite motifs. So I set what I had begun to cut aside, and instead cut repeat sections from the other lengthwise half and got beautiful blocks from my favorite part of the fabric.

4. Take time to choose the right pattern for the fabric. There is an old saying for carpenters, "Measure twice and cut once." So when you are gripped by the excitement of diving into a new project, slow down a bit and think about the quilt you want to make. Which size triangle or diamond will bring out the best in the fabric pattern you are working with? In this book are more than 50 patterns to choose from. Page through and visualize your fabric in a variety of block patterns.

5. Do it with mirrors. Joan has two small mirrors taped together so they open like a book. Open it to 60° using the Super 60™ and tape or glue a thread in position so it won't open farther. Then set this opened mirror book on the fabric for a preview of the designs you will get from sets of stacked fabric. This is not quite right, because every other section is reversed, which does not happen with the actual fabric. But if you don't like surprises, this might be for you. *(see title page)*

6. Instead of stacking your fabric with pins, use a needle and thread. Put the point of the needle through a particular spot as you would a pin. When all six layers are lined up correctly, take a small tight stitch (less than ¼") through all the layers. Add a couple more stitches or backstitches to lock the fabric in position. Though it takes a little more patience at the beginning, this is easy to press and cut as you create your stacked sets.

7. Cut your first repeat set, whether diamonds or triangles, and lay it out to see how it looks. Then choose the accent colors and other fabrics for that block. As you make more blocks, you may add other fabrics to your quilt. *(Iron the first repeat set onto wax paper, or baste it together, and take it to the fabric store with you to choose more fabrics.)*

8. Putting wedges together may be easier and more accurate if you press the seams up/down on alternate wedges. Butted seams line up well!

THE FUSSY CUT

In the past, to achieve a kaleidoscope effect, individual shapes have been chosen and cut one at a time from a single layer of fabric. The resulting design tends to be static, tight and controlled. This kind of precision can sparkle like a gemstone. This technique is especially useful when identical motifs are printed close to each other over the fabric, but offset, so cutting a strip would destroy many motifs.

The quilter cuts a template the shape and size desired from template plastic. Position this shape on the fabric to get the most attractive design. Mark around the template with washout marker, pencil, or a ballpoint pen. Cut with a scissors inside the marked lines. Instead of cutting single diamonds or triangles, you can stack fabrics first, and then cut six identical, carefully chosen motifs at the same time, without cutting a strip. This way you can cut your shape in any direction.

WHICH BLOCK DESIGN?

Once you have narrowed this project down to just one wonderful print, you must decide which block design suits this fabric. A determining factor will be the scale of the motifs in the print. Is it a 2" butterfly floating on a background with lots of space between each one? Or is it a 5" tropical flower with leaves swirling in the spaces between?

One way to anticipate repeat results is to simply lay the Super 60™ on the fabric and look at what is inside the triangle. Even with much planning and thought, you will still be surprised by the designs formed by stacked pattern repeats. Once you have an idea of the desired scale of the pattern repeat, you can look for those block designs using the best size of triangle or diamond and make a choice among them.

MY APPROACH

Making a Serendipity quilt is a lot of fun. When I have a beautiful repeat fabric picked out, I'm eager to begin stacking and cutting. I pull a group of accent fabrics and dive in! Seldom am I completely satisfied with the first block. Usually I try something different next. After about half the blocks are made, I plan blocks to go well with what I already have. In the end, I have an assortment of blocks that I pull together with the arrangement of the blocks, background fabrics, borders, etc. One advantage of this way of piecing quilts is that I get to try many possibilities and use most of them. These quilts have a painterly look that draws the eye first to one detail and then another in a pleasing visual experience. My art training and years of quilting help me to be successful in this eclectic approach.

AN ARTIST'S STATEMENT
Virginia Anderson

The key to my picking fabrics is patience, many trips to the fabric stores, a willingness to buy more fabrics than I will ever use in that particular quilt, and to let a quilt sit in a box while I continue to add to the fabrics over a long period of time. I visit fabric shops often, always on the lookout for a fabric find that just sings to me. "Buy me!" Usually I buy ⅜ yard of a fabric. If it's singing really loud, three yards. Then I will keep my eyes open for the perfect quilt pattern to go with it. Sometimes I begin with the quilt pattern, and look for the perfect fabric.

I carry a swatch of fabric to quilt shops. I put fabrics up on my quilt wall and think about them before I begin to cut. The fabrics are considered as long as necessary, I **never** make the choice of just picking some fabric to get the decision done. For example, I have a quilt in mind that I have been working on, choosing fabrics for, for about four years. I think I have probably bought 25 yards total of different background fabrics till I finally found the combination that I am actually using. What matters is what's best for the quilt.

In choosing fabrics specifically for the Serendipity quilts, I will carry the mirrors with me in my hunt for the perfect focus fabric. It not only has to look good repeated, but I have to like it. I do look at the "character" of the fabrics, the design of the pattern, and try to keep it related to the main fabric both in tone and design.

I sew a very first test block and begin to choose supporting fabrics. I may not use that first block, but learn from it. When piecing each block, I use the mirror to see exactly what I am getting in the way of a repeat motif. I find that by using the mirrors I can get the best use of the fabric design, more variety and better interest in the featured blocks.

I spend a lot of time beforehand just playing with what is available. This process is continuous until all the center repeats are cut out and on the wall, as I continue to make decisions. I prefer to have a huge fabric palette some of which I do not end up using. Even if I am in the middle of making blocks, I am still looking for fabric to supplement my choices or substitute for less desirable fabrics. I make more blocks and setting triangles than I end up using. When I finish the quilt top there are various pieced triangles that are extra and also those that I pieced that ended up wrong colors or combinations of color etc.

Visual Index Of Shapes To Cut

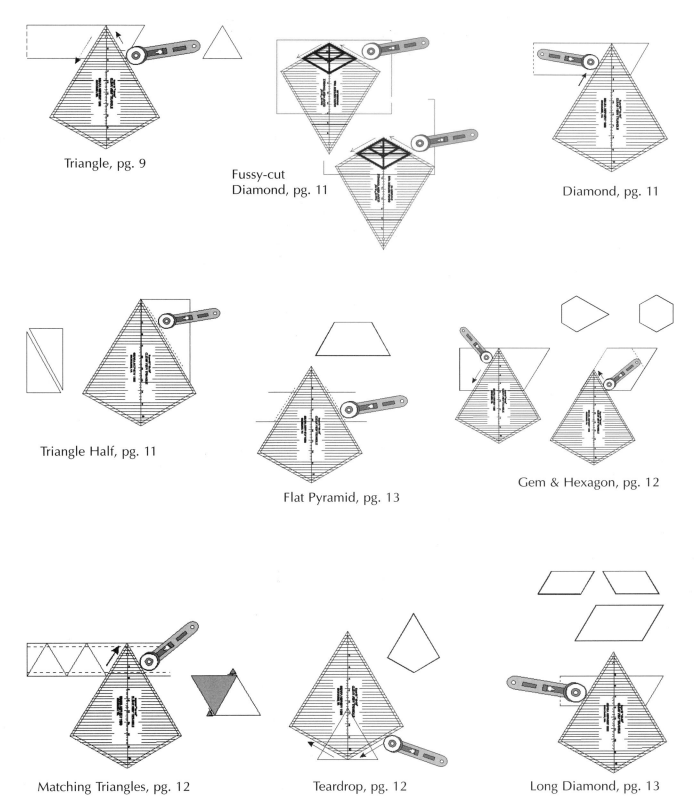

Triangle, pg. 9

Fussy-cut
Diamond, pg. 11

Diamond, pg. 11

Triangle Half, pg. 11

Flat Pyramid, pg. 13

Gem & Hexagon, pg. 12

Matching Triangles, pg. 12

Teardrop, pg. 12

Long Diamond, pg. 13

CUTTING DIRECTIONS

TOOLS

This book features the Super 60™. The Super 60 combines the most versatile Clearview Triangle, the 8" Mini-Pro, with the ½-diamond, so with one tool you can cut every shape needed in this book. (Sometimes a cut will need to be extended with a straight ruler to make a larger piece.)

Both the Super 60 and all the Clearview Triangles are made from ⅛" thick acrylic for use with a rotary cutter. (See pg. 112 for ordering information.) You may already own the two tools mentioned above. If so, you will not need the new tool. Just use the 8" triangle when directions refer to "the narrow end" and the ½-diamond when directions refer to "the wide end".

Besides the Super 60 or Clearview Triangles, required tools are: a rotary cutter, a mat, and a straight ruler like Omnigrid for cutting strips. Use the size of rotary cutter you prefer, although the smallest is better for cutting around curves (like cutting out clothing patterns), and the two larger sizes save muscle strain, cut faster, and tend to stay on a straight line. A 6" x 12" ruler moves less while cutting.

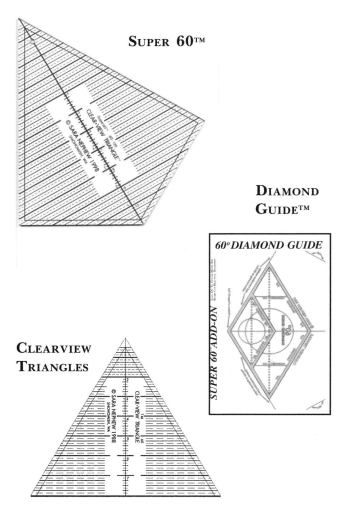

SUPER 60™

DIAMOND GUIDE™

THE DIAMOND GUIDE

This new static cling label can be added onto the wide end of the Super 60 and used as a guide for fussy-cutting two sizes of diamonds and a hexagon. Two colors are included, red and white, so the guide-lines will show up well on any color of fabric. When not in use, the static cling label can be returned to its backing and kept in the package. A pattern is included.

CLEARVIEW TRIANGLES

ROTARY CUTTING AND SPEED-PIECING

These cutting methods are based on:
1. a strip of fabric;
2. a plastic 60° triangle tool with a ruled line on the perpendicular. The tool is laid on the strip in various ways, and a rotary cutter is used to cut off portions of the fabric strip. Nothing in this book is difficult to do as long as the triangle tool and the strip are kept in mind. By working just with these elements, many shapes can be cut in whatever size is desired. These shapes will all fit together to form a quilt top. The following section lists the methods for cutting the shapes used in this book.

OMNIGRID™ 6" x 12"

OLFA™ CUTTER

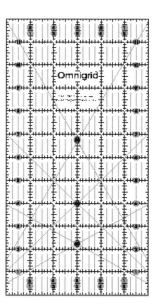

Piecing Hints

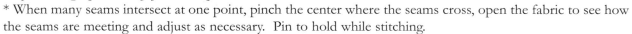

* All my piecing is done with a ¼" seam. Check the seams occasionally until you are confident of accuracy. Be sure the seam is just inside the ¼" line rather than right on it.

Note : More and more, I twist seams to allow seam intersections to butt up against each other, making points come together well and reducing bulk. Where a seam triangle sticks out past the fabric edge, press away from this point in both directions.

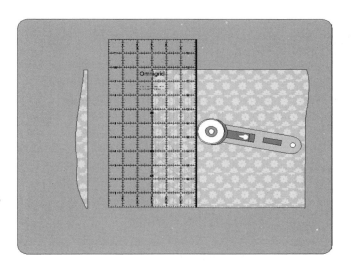

Pressed out to reduce bulk

* When many seams intersect at one point, pinch the center where the seams cross, open the fabric to see how the seams are meeting and adjust as necessary. Pin to hold while stitching.

* Do not trim off the little 60° points that stick out past the fabric edge. They are very useful to help align the units for accurate sewing. Only trim them after the top is pieced if they will show through a light fabric.

* The mild bias of the 60° triangle aids in lining up seams. Pull a little if necessary. All seams are pressed to one side to make the quilt top durable. Press from the top with a wet press cloth.

To Cut A Strip

To cut a strip:

The first step in cutting any shape is to cut a strip. All fabric should be prewashed. 100% cotton is best.

1. Fold fabric selvage-to-selvage and press. If pressing from the selvage to the fold produces wrinkles, move the top layer of fabric left or right keeping selvages parallel, until wrinkles disappear.
2. Bring fold to selvage (folding again) and press.
3. Use the wide ruler as a right angle guide, or line up the selvages with the edge of the mat, and the ruler with the mat edge perpendicular to the selvage. Cut off the ragged or irregular edges of the fabric.
4. Cut the strip width required, using the newly trimmed fabric edge as a guide.
5. Open the strip. It should be straight, not zigzag. Adjust the ruler if necessary and trim fabric edges slightly before cutting the next strip.

Trim ragged edge from twice-folded fabric. Then begin to cut strips. Use a wide ruler (or lines on the mat) to line up cuts.

Pieces To Cut-- Triangle

To cut a triangle (3½" triangle size):

1. Cut a 3½" strip (or a strip the size of the triangle).
2. Position the narrow end of the Super 60 at one edge of the strip and the 3½" line (or the line the size of the triangle) at the other edge of the strip.
3. Rotary cut along both sides of the triangle. Move the tool along the same edge (do not flip it to the other side of the fabric strip) for the next cut. Line up the tool again as shown.
4. Cut along both sides of the triangle. Strips may be stacked up to 8 thicknesses and all cut at once.

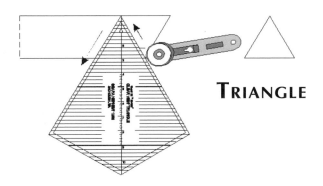

Triangle

FUSSY-CUT DIAMONDS

Fussy-cut diamonds and other shapes can be chosen and cut one at a time from a single layer of fabric. The result tends to be static, tighter and more controlled than a stacked repeat. Fussy-cut repeats can create designs as precise and sparkling as a gemstone. Somewhat more fabric will be wasted by cutting only these selected designs from the whole fabric.

OR: Instead of cutting single diamonds, you can stack fabrics first, and then cut six identical, carefully chosen diamonds at the same time.

THE OLD-FASHIONED WAY

Cut a template the shape and size desired from template plastic. Position this shape on the fabric to get the most attractive design. You will most likely be wasting some fabric, but beauty is the desired result, not thrift. Mark around the template with washout marker, pencil, or a ballpoint pen that you know washes out. Cut with a scissors on the marked lines.

A FASTER WAY

The author likes to rotary cut everything, and trying to draw an outline and then cut it out got tiring very quickly! So she made a guide for rotary cutting as follows: Cut a diamond (or other shape) the size needed from a full-page computer label. Cut out a smaller diamond (or other shape) inside the first, so the ¼" outline of the shape remains. Peel and stick the label diamond on the 120° end of the Super 60™, (if a triangle, on the 60° end) as a guide for centering a motif to be rotary cut. Establish a lengthwise center line by sticking on a narrow strip of the label paper down the inside center of the diamond outline. Note: When you remove the label, a little kerosene or charcoal starter fluid on a rag will clean sticker glue off without damaging the rulings. When using the rotary cutter, try not to extend the cuts farther than necessary, in order to preserve the rest of the fabric. *OR : Use the Diamond Guide™ available from Clearview Triangle for two sizes of 60° diamonds and a 3¼" hexagon. See pg. 112 for ordering information.*

GUIDE FOR TRIANGLES

Cut out triangles with the desired motif using a rotary cutter and the 60° end of the Super 60™. Use a strip of tape or computer label to show where the bottom of the triangle will be.

DIAMOND GUIDE™

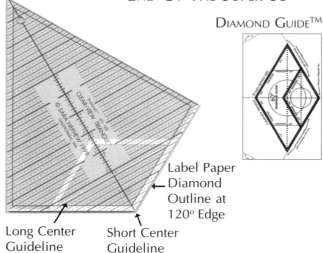

Label Paper Diamond Outline at 120° Edge

Long Center Guideline   Short Center Guideline

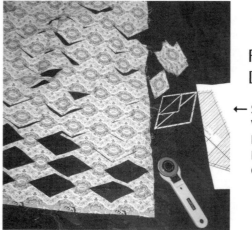

FUSSY-CUT DIAMONDS

← Super 60™ With A Handmade Diamond Guide

Example: cutting 1⅞" diamonds to make small stars. The motifs are all cut along two sides of the diamond first. Then the fabric is turned, and the other two sides are cut. Only every other motif can be used, since the cuts extend into the space in between.

Fussy-cut repeats in a diamond make a star to use in a Setting Triangle

DIAMOND

To cut a diamond (3½" triangle size) :

1. Cut a 3¼" strip (or size the directions call for).
2. Position the Super 60 (narrow end up) with one side along one edge of the strip. Cut the end of the strip to a 60° angle.
3. Reposition so the tip is at one edge of the strip and a ruled line along the other edge (same position asused to cut triangles, except the strip is ¼" narrower).
4. Rotary cut **only** along the side opposite the first cut.
5. Keep moving the tool along the same side of the strip, lining up the cut edge and the side of the tool as shown. Always cut the side opposite the first cut. (Strips may be stacked up to 8 thicknesses and all cut at once.)

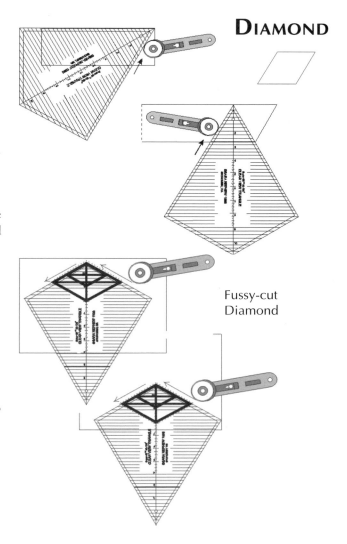

Fussy-cut
Diamond

FUSSY-CUT DIAMOND

To fussy-cut a diamond:

1. Center the motif in the diamond and cut along two sides of the diamond on either side of the wide angle first. Then turn the fabric and cut the other two sides. Only every other motif can be used since the cuts extend into the space in between. Try not to extend the cuts farther than necessary in order to preserve the rest of the fabric.

TRIANGLE HALF

To cut a triangle half (3½" triangle size):
Method #1

1. Cut triangles from a 4" strip.
2. Line up the side of the fabric triangle with the perpendicular line on the narrow end of the Super 60. Cut the fabric triangle in half along the edge of the tool.

Method #2

1. Cut a rectangle the height and width needed for the triangle half as given in the directions (ex. 2⅜" x 4").
2. Using the narrow end of the Super 60, bisect this rectangle from corner-to-corner diagonally. (This will produce two halves the same, rather than a left and a right. Lay the ruler from corner-to-corner to check and see if this is the shape needed. If not, lay it along the other two corners. To get left and right halves, lay two rectangles right or wrong sides together.)

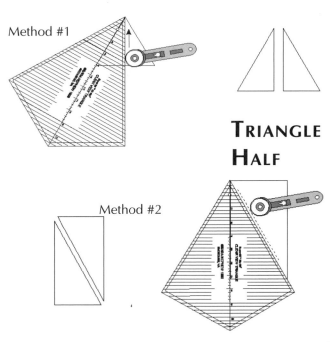

Method #1

Method #2

TRIANGLE HALF

Hexagon & Gem

HEXAGON

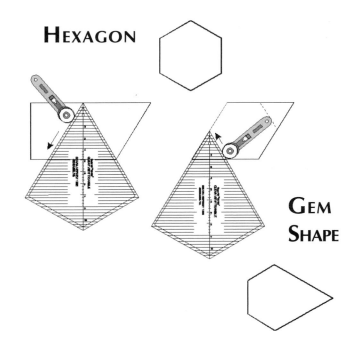

To cut a hexagon:
1. Cut a 3¼" strip (6" for the whole hexagon in a setting triangle).
2. Cut 60° diamonds from the strip. (See "To cut a diamond," on pg. 11.)
3. From each end of the diamond, cut a 1⅝" triangle (3" for setting triangle hexagon).

To cut a gem shape:
Instead of cutting a hexagon from the diamond, cut only one point off, leaving the gem shape.

GEM SHAPE

Matching Triangles

(Sandwich-Piecing uses two strips of fabric.)
To sandwich-piece a matching triangle (3½" triangle size):
1. Cut 3½" strips. (Strip width is always the same as the triangle size.) Two different fabrics are used, usually one light and one dark. Seam these strips right sides together with a ¼" seam down both the right and the left side of the pair of strips. Cut triangles from this set of strips.
2. Pull the tips of the seamed triangles apart and press.

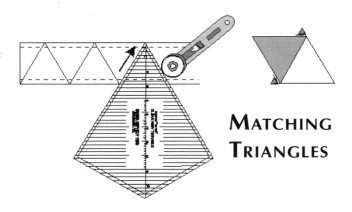

MATCHING TRIANGLES

Teardrop

To cut a teardrop (3½" triangle size):
Method #1
1. Cut triangles from strip size given in the directions.
2. Position the Super 60 on the triangle upside down and centered, with the perpendicular line on the top point of the triangle, the other two triangle points lined up evenly with one of the rulings, and the wide angle just at or inside the bottom edge as shown. Cut excess from the base of the teardrop.

Method #2 (Using a Clearview Triangle)
1. Cut triangles from a strip.
2. Measure the base of these triangles and find the center or half measurement.
3. Lay the perpendicular of the triangle tool along the base of the fabric triangle with the point at center. Rotary cut this wedge off. Reverse the tool and cut off the other wedge.

TEARDROP

Method #1

Method #2

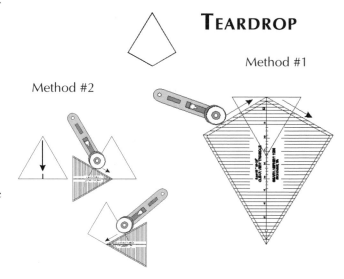

LONG DIAMOND

To cut a long diamond (3½" triangle size):
1. Cut strip width as required in the pattern.
2. Trim one end of the strip to a 60° angle.
3. Place the Super 60 over the fabric strip as shown. Set the bottom edge of the strip at the measurement given in the pattern. Cut the side opposite the first cut.

Or:
1. After cutting the correct width strip, trim it to a 60° angle as in #1 and #2 above.
2. Use a straight ruler to cut the correct width parallel to the angled end.

Long diamonds do have a reverse of their shape. Check carefully to be sure you are cutting them in the direction required by the pattern.

LONG DIAMOND

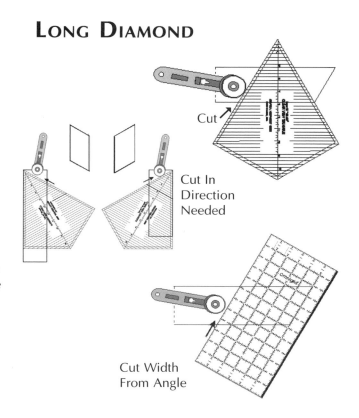

Cut

Cut In Direction Needed

Cut Width From Angle

FLAT PYRAMID

To cut a flat pyramid (3½" triangle size):
1. Cut a 3¼" strip (or size the directions call for).
2. Place the narrow end of the Super 60 over the fabric strip, lining up the bottom edge of the strip at the measurement given in the pattern (often 6¼"). Cut on both sides of the tool.
3. Turn the Super 60 and cut the next flat pyramid from the other side of the strip to save fabric.

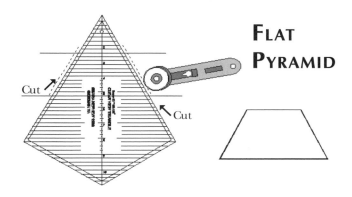

Cut

Cut

FLAT PYRAMID

STRIP-PIECED TRIANGLES

Some of these designs can be speeded up by sewing strips together first, and then cutting triangles from the strip. A few piecing tips will help to improve accuracy and and give a look of crisp precision. Of course, careful cutting of the strips is important. In addition:
1. Sometimes it helps to always begin sewing at the same edge of the strip set.
2. Press to the dark if possible.
3. Press across the strip set, from the back, and pull it as wide as possible to make sure there is no fabric folded into the seam.
4. Then press the strip from the front, lengthwise, pulling to make the set of strips straight. Use a wet press cloth if you wish.

STRIP-PIECED LONG DIAMONDS & REVERSE

Cut a light and a dark 3¼" strip. Sew together lengthwise. Fold right sides together or make two strip sets and place right sides together, do not butt the seams, but place light to light, and dark to dark. Trim the strip set to a 60° angle, then cut 1⅞" sections from the strip set. Check the 60° angle often.

Blocks To Choose From

Hint: The smaller center repeat shapes are easier to work with, but larger shapes can produce exceptional results.

VISUAL INDEX OF SERENDIPITY BLOCKS

In Alphabetical Order

Balance
pg. 67

Big Star
pg. 81

Bigtooth
pg. 24

Big Triangle
pg. 19

Blooming
pg. 68

Botanical
pg. 40

Brilliant Sky
pg. 37

Budding
pg. 71

Cactus Flower
pg. 30

Candle
pg. 34

Dark Feather
pg. 76

Echo Feather
pg. 77

Expanding Star
pg. 46

Expanding
Star Variation
pg. 47

Feather
pg. 36

Fern pg. 39

Fin pg. 80

Fish pg. 72

Frozen Roses
pg. 35

Gull
pg. 73

Hearts
pg. 74

Ice Crystal
pg. 38

Log Petal
pg. 26

Lotus Flower
pg. 78

Mariner's
Delight pg. 22

Moonscape
pg. 33

Nested Hearts
pg. 43

Petal
pg. 82

Pinwheel
pg. 69

Popcorn
pg. 44

Prickley Pear
pg. 28

Ribbon
pg. 66

Rose Pinwheel
pg. 70

Seashell
pg. 17

Sheriff's Star
pg. 48

Silk Stocking
pg. 41

Simple Crochet
pg. 75

Snowfall
pg. 23

Sparkling Sky
pg. 65

Sunrise
pg. 32

Texas Sunflower
pg. 16

Thimble Star
pg. 18

Tooth
pg. 83

Torch
pg. 42

Trim
pg. 84

Watercrystal
pg. 27

Wedge Circle
pg. 20

Wedge Star
pg. 21

Wings Of A Dove
pg. 45

Not Shown - Beanie   pg. 85

Texas Sunflower

1. Cut for one block:

12	medium	2⅛"	triangle
24	dark	2⅛"	triangle
18	light	1⅞"	diamond
6	center*	3½"	triangle
6	dark	3½"	triangle
12	light	3¼"	diamond

All cutting is based on the 3½" triangle size.

From a design by Claudine McGee

2. Sew one light 1⅞" diamond and two medium 2⅛" triangles into a pieced triangle as shown. Make six of these.(A) Make 12 with dark triangles. (B)

3. Assemble three pieced triangles (one A, 2 B) from #2 above plus a center triangle, two light diamonds, and a dark triangle to make one wedge. Make six of these.

4. Sew the wedges three and three and sew across the middle to make a hexagon block.

Pieced Triangles

A.   B.

Wedge Piecing
Diagram

One Wedge

Texas Sunflower Block

Cinco De Mayo Quilt

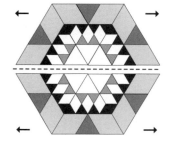

Piecing Diagram
Press seams away
from center
Pinch and pin center

SEASHELLS

All cutting is based on the 3½" triangle size.

Directions:

2. Sew one center triangle and one flat pyramid into a stripped triangle as shown. Sew two light diamonds and one dark triangle into a pieced strip as shown. Sew the triangle and the strip together to make one wedge. Make six of these.

3. Sew the wedges together into two sets of three. Line up and pin the centers and sew all the way across to join the two halves and complete the hexagon block.

1. Cut for one block:

1.	6	center*	3½"	triangle
2.	12	light	3¼"	diamond
3.	6	dark	3½"	triangle
4.	6	medium	6¼"	flat pyramid
				from 3¼" strip

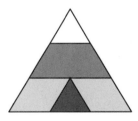

← *Repeat Fabric*

Wedge Piecing Diagram

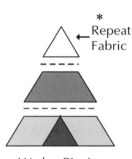

One Wedge

SEASHELLS BLOCK

SEASHELLS QUILT

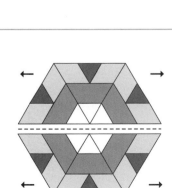

PIECING DIAGRAM
Press seams away from center
Pinch and pin center

Thimble Star

Directions:

2. Sew one medium diamond and two light triangles into a pieced triangle. Sew a light and dark long diamond together vertically as shown. Do the same with the reverse long diamonds. (Or sew a dark and light 3¼" strip together lengthwise, fold right sides together, trim to a 60o angle, and cut 1⅞" widths from the stripset.) Sew the long diamond sets left and right of the pieced triangle to make a pieced flat pyramid. Sew the center triangle on top of this to make one wedge. Make six of these.

3. Sew the wedges together into two sets of three. Pinch and pin and sew all the way across to join the two halves and complete the hexagon block.

Pieced Triangle

Wedge Piecing Diagram

* Repeat Fabric ←

One Wedge

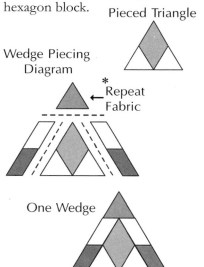

Thimble Star Block

1. Cut for one block:

1.	6 center* and 12 light	3½"	triangle
2.	6 medium	3¼"	diamond
3.	6 light and 6 dark	3¼"	long diamond
4.	6 light(reverse)		cut from a 1⅞" strip
5.	6 dark(reverse)		(or strip-piece these)

Valentine Lace Quilt

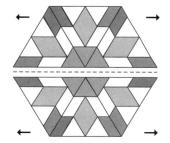

Piecing Diagram
Press seams away from center
Pinch and pin center

18

Big Triangle

1. Cut for one block:

1.	6	center*	3½"	triangle
2.	12	light	3½"	flat pyramid from 1⅞" strip
3.	6	dark	3¼"	diamond
4.	12	med	4⅞"	triangle

All cutting is based on the 3½" triangle size.

Directions:

2. Use a center triangle, two light flat pyramids, a dark diamond, and two medium triangles to make one wedge. Make six of these.

3. Sew the wedges three and three and sew across the middle to complete the hexagon block.

← Repeat
Fabric

Wedge Piecing Diagram

One Wedge

BIG TRIANGLE BLOCK

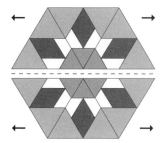

PIECING DIAGRAM
Press seams away from center
Pinch and pin center

Wedge Circle

Directions:

2. Sew one dark triangle and the medium 6¼" flat pyramid into a stripped triangle as shown. Sew a light and dark long diamond together vertically as shown. Do the same with the reverse long diamonds. (Or sew a dark and light 3¼" strip together lengthwise, fold right sides together, trim to a 60° angle, and cut 1⅞" widths from the stripset.) Sew the long diamond sets left and right of the stripped triangle to make a pieced flat pyramid. Sew the center triangle on top of this to make one wedge. Make six.

3. Sew the wedges together into two sets of three. Pinch and pin and sew all the way across to join the two halves and complete the hexagon block.

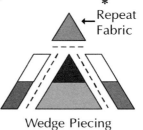

Wedge Piecing Diagram

One Wedge

WEDGE CIRCLE BLOCK

1. Cut for one block:

1.	6 center* and 6 dark	3½"	triangle
2.	6 medium (3¼" strip)	6¼"	flat pyramid
3.	6 light and 6 dark	3¼"	long diamond
4.	6 light(reverse)		cut from a 1⅞" strip
5.	6 dark(reverse)		(or strip-piece these)

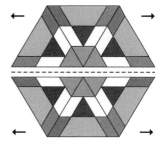

PIECING DIAGRAM
Press seams away from center
Pinch and pin center

20

WEDGE STAR

Directions:

2. Sew a light and dark long diamond together vertically as shown. Do the same with the reverse long diamonds. (Or sew a dark and light 3¼" strip together lengthwise, fold right sides together, trim to a 60° angle, and cut 1⅞" widths from the stripset.) Sew the long diamond sets left and right of the 6¼" triangle to make a pieced flat pyramid. Sew the center triangle on top of this to make one wedge. Make six of these.

3. Sew the wedges together into two sets of three. Pinch and pin and sew all the way across to join the two halves and complete the hexagon block.

1. Cut for one block:

1.	6	center*	3½"	triangle
2.	6	medium	6¼"	triangle
3.	6	light and dark	3¼"	long diamond
4.	6	light and dark (reverse)		from 1⅞" strip

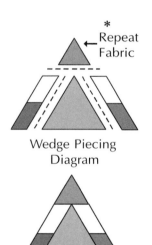

Wedge Piecing Diagram

One Wedge

WEDGE STAR BLOCK

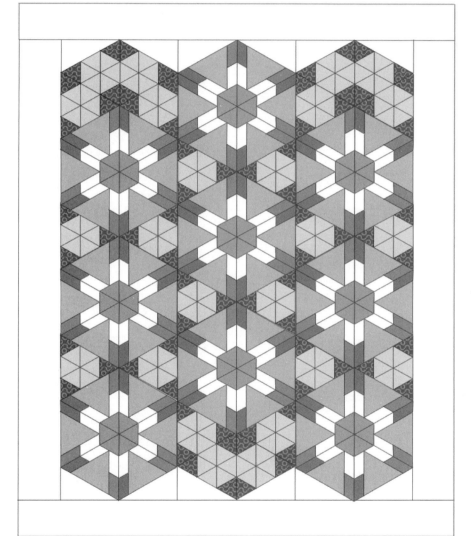

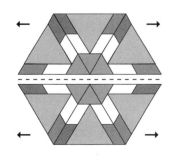

PIECING DIAGRAM
Press seams away from center
Pinch and pin center

Mariner's Delight

Directions:

2. Cut a light and dark 2⅛" strip and sew them together lengthwise. Cut 3¾" triangles from this set of strips. Cut off a ¼" strip from the bottom of each of these stripped triangles.

3. Sew two dark-tipped stripped triangles to the dark triangle as shown. Sew two dark-based stripped triangles to the medium flat pyramid as shown. Sew these two units together with a center triangle at the top to make one wedge. Make six of these.

4. Sew the wedges three and three and sew across the middle to complete the hexagon block.

1. Cut for one block:

1.	6	center*	3½"	triangle
2.	6	dark	3½"	triangle
3.	6	medium	6¼"	flat pyramid (from 3¼" strip)

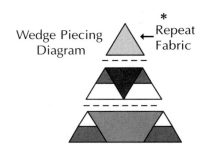

Wedge Piecing Diagram

*←Repeat Fabric

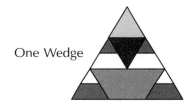

One Wedge

MARINER'S DELIGHT BLOCK

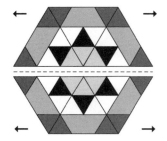

PIECING DIAGRAM
Press seams away
from center
Pinch and pin center

SNOWFALL

1. Cut for one block:

1.	6	center*	3½"	triangle
2.	12	light	3½"	triangle
3.	12	dark	3½"	triangle
4.	12	dark	4⅞"	flat pyramid (from 3¼" strip)

Directions:

2. Assemble a center triangle, two light triangles, two dark triangles, and two flat pyramids to make one wedge. Make six of these.

4. Sew the wedges three and three and sew across the middle to complete the hexagon block.

All cutting is based on the 3½" triangle size.

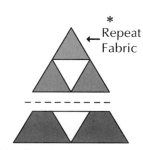

* ← Repeat Fabric

Wedge Piecing Diagram

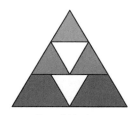

One Wedge

SNOWFALL BLOCK

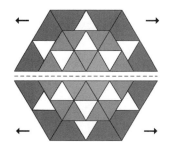

PIECING DIAGRAM
Press seams away from center
Pinch and pin center

23

BIGTOOTH

Directions:

1. *Please see note about stripped triangles on pg. 13.* Cut a light and dark 2⅛" strip and sew them together lengthwise. Cut 3¾" triangles from this set of strips. Cut off a ¼" strip from the bottom of each of these stripped triangles. (You will get both light- and dark-based triangles from this set of strips. Choose one kind, and set the other kind aside for a different quilt, or make some blocks using the other kind of triangles.)

2. Cut for one block:

1.	6	center*	3½"	triangle
2.	12	dark	2⅛"	triangle
3.	6	light	1⅞"	diamond
4.	6	light	3¼"	long diamond
5.	6	light (reverse)		(1⅞" strip)

3. Sew a 1⅞" diamond and two 2⅛" triangles into a pieced triangle as shown. Assemble with two stripped triangles to make a pieced flat pyramid as shown (A).

4. Sew three stripped triangles into another pieced flat pyramid (B). Add the light long diamond and the light reverse long diamond left and right. Sew pyramid (A) on top of pyramid (B) and add the 3½" triangle to complete one wedge. Make six of these.

5. Sew the wedges together into two sets of three. Pinch and pin and sew all the way across to join the two halves and complete the hexagon block.

BIGTOOTH STAR BLOCK LIGHT

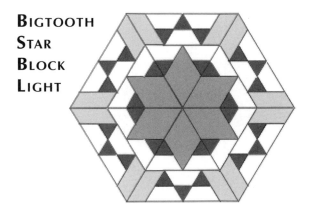

Many variations of this design are possible. The block above is Bigtooth Light, with a 3¼" center* diamond substituted in place of the pieced triangle and the center* triangle. This could be done in the Bigfoot block with all dark-based triangles also. What would happen if you used both dark-based and light-based stripped triangles in the same block? Where would you put each of them?

Pieced Triangle

Pieced Flat Pyramid

A.

Pieced Flat Pyramid

B.

*
← Repeat Fabric

Wedge Piecing Diagram

One Wedge

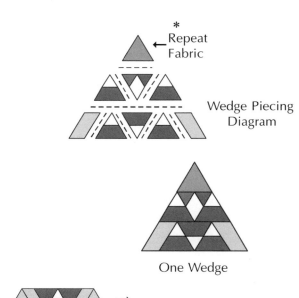

PIECING DIAGRAM
Press seams away from center
Pinch and pin center

BIGTOOTH

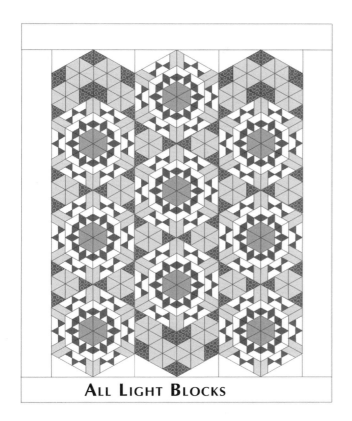

ALL LIGHT BLOCKS

ALL DARK BLOCKS

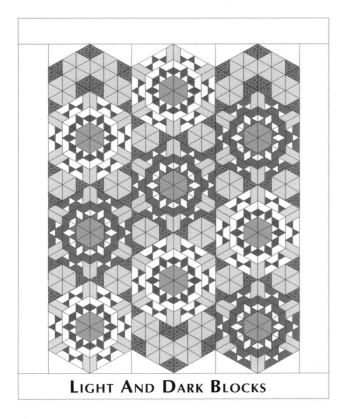

LIGHT AND DARK BLOCKS

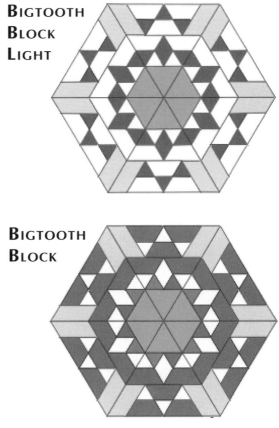

BIGTOOTH BLOCK LIGHT

BIGTOOTH BLOCK

Log Petal

1. Cut for one block:

1.	6	center*	3½"	triangle
2	6	medium	3¼"	diamond
3.	12	dark	3½"	triangle
4.	12	light	3½"	flat pyramid
5.	12	light	4⅞"	from a 1⅞" strip

Directions:

2. Sew two 3½" flat pyramids on either side of one end of a diamond as shown. Then sew the 4⅞" flat pyramid on either side of the other end. Sew on the two dark triangles and the center* triangle as shown to complete one wedge. Make six of these.

3. Sew the wedges together into two sets of three. Pinch and pin and sew all the way across to join the two halves and complete the hexagon block.

Sew On Flat Pyramids

Wedge Piecing Diagram

* Repeat Fabric

One Wedge

Log Petal Block

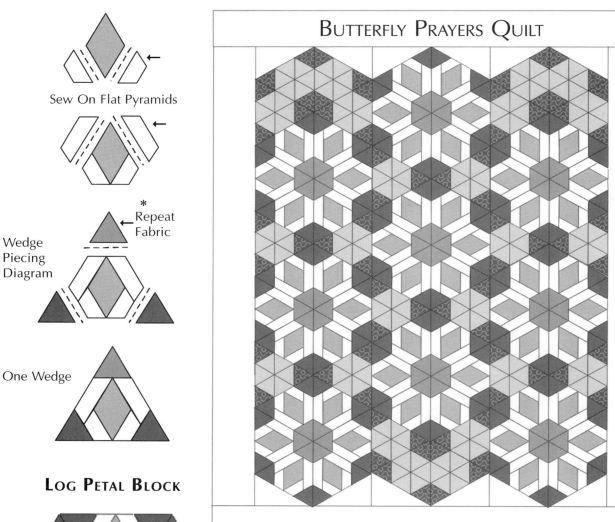

Butterfly Prayers Quilt

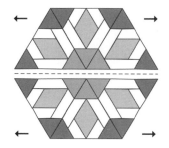

Piecing Diagram
Press seams away from center
Pinch and pin center

WATERCRYSTAL

1. Cut for one block:

1.	6	center*	3½"	triangle
2.	18	dark	3½"	triangle
3.	12	light	3½"	triangle
4.	6	medium	6¼"	flat pyramid from 3¼" strip

All cutting is based on the 3½" triangle size.

Directions:

2. Use a center triangle, three dark triangles, two light triangles, and one flat pyramid to make one wedge. Make six of these.

3. Sew the wedges three and three and sew across the middle to complete the hexagon block.

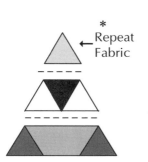

* Repeat Fabric

Wedge Piecing Diagram

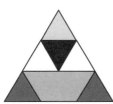

One Wedge

WATERCRYSTAL BLOCK

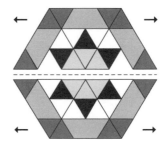

PIECING DIAGRAM
Press seams away from center
Pinch and pin center

Prickly Pear

Directions:

1. *Please see note about stripped triangles on pg. 13.* Cut a light and dark 2⅛" strip and sew them together lengthwise. Cut 3¾" triangles from this set of strips. Cut off a ¼" strip from the bottom of each of these stripped triangles. (You will get both light and dark-based triangles from this set of strips. Choose one kind, and set the other kind aside for a different quilt, or make some blocks using the other kind of triangles.)

2. Cut for one block:

1.	6	light	1⅞"	diamond
2.	12	dark	2⅛"	triangle
3.	6	center*	3½"	triangle
4.	6	dark		
5.	12	light	4⅞"	flat pyramid from 3¼" strip

3. Sew one light 1⅞" diamond and two medium 2⅛" triangles into a pieced triangle as shown.

4. Use one pieced triangle from #3 above, plus two dark-based stripped triangles to make a pieced Unit A.

5. Use a dark triangle and two flat pyramids to make a pieced Unit B.

6. Combine a center* triangle, pieced Unit A and pieced Unit B to make one wedge. Make six of these. Sew the wedges three and three and sew across the middle to make a hexagon block.

Pieced Triangle

Pieced Unit A

Pieced Unit B

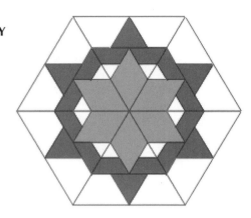

PRICKLY PEAR STAR BLOCK

Many variations of this design are possible. The block above is Prickly Pear Star, with a 3¼" center* diamond substituted in place of the pieced triangle and the center* triangle. This could be done in the Prickly Pear block with all light-based triangles also. What would happen if you used both dark-based and light-based stripped triangles in the same block? Where would you put them?

*
← Repeat Fabric

Wedge Piecing Diagram

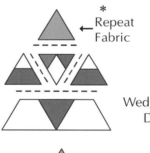

One Wedge

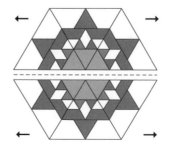

PIECING DIAGRAM
Press seams away from center
Pinch and pin center

PRICKLY PEAR

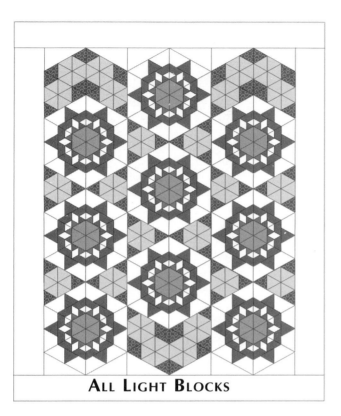

ALL LIGHT BLOCKS

ALL DARK BLOCKS

LIGHT AND DARK BLOCKS

PRICKLEY
PEAR
BLOCK
WITH
VALUES
REVERSED

PRICKLEY
PEAR
BLOCK

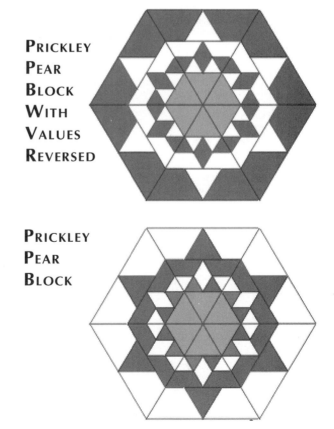

CACTUS FLOWER

All cutting is based on the 3½" triangle size.

Directions:

1. Cut a light and dark 2⅛" strip and sew them together lengthwise. Cut 3¾" triangles from this set of strips. Cut off a ¼" strip from the bottom of each of these stripped triangles. (You will get both light and dark-based triangles from this set of strips. Choose one kind, and set the other kind aside for a different quilt, or make some blocks in this quilt using the other kind of triangles. *Please see note about stripped triangles on pg. 13.*)

2. Cut a light and dark 1⅞" strip and sew them together lengthwise. Cut 4⅞" flat pyramids from this set of strips. (You will get both light and dark-based flat pyramids from this set of strips. Choose one kind, and set the other kind aside for a different quilt, or make some blocks using the other kind of flat pyramids.)

3. In addition, cut for one block:

1.	6	dark	1⅞"	diamond
2.	12	light	2⅛"	triangle
3.	6	center*	3½"	triangle

4. Sew a 1⅞" diamond and two 2⅛" triangles into a pieced triangle as shown. Assemble with two stripped triangles to make a pieced unit (A).

Pieced Triangle   B.   Pieced Unit A

5. Sew a stripped triangle and two stripped flat pyramids into a pieced unit (B). Sew onto (A) as shown and add the 3½" triangle to complete one wedge. Make six of these.

Pieced Unit B

6. Sew the wedges together into two sets of three. Pinch and pin and sew all the way across to join the two halves and complete the hexagon block.

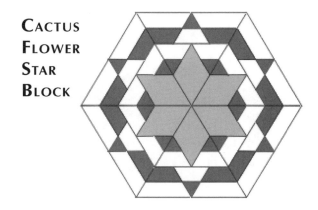

CACTUS FLOWER STAR BLOCK

Many variations of this design are possible. The block above is Cactus Flower Star, with a 3¼" center* diamond substituted in place of the pieced triangle and the center* triangle. This could be done in the Cactus Flower block with all dark-based triangles also. What would happen if you used both dark-based and light-based stripped triangles or stripped flat pyramids in the same block? Where would you put them?

*
← Repeat Fabric

Wedge Piecing Diagram

One Wedge

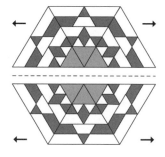

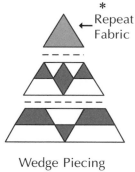

PIECING DIAGRAM
Press seams away from center
Pinch and pin center

30

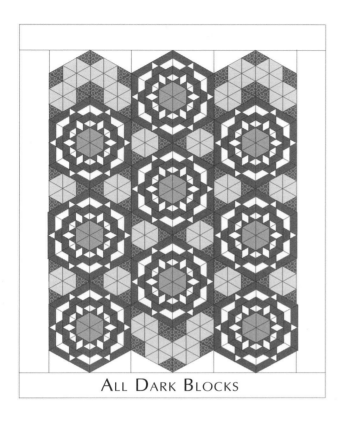

ALL DARK BLOCKS

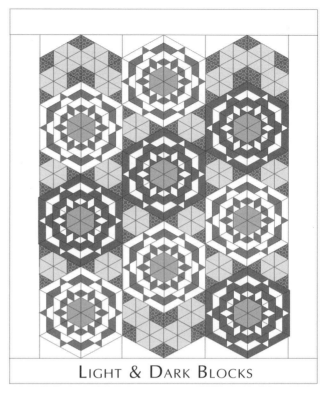

LIGHT & DARK BLOCKS

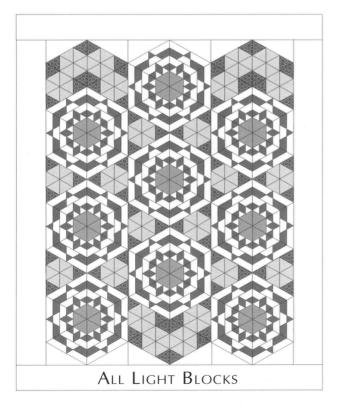

ALL LIGHT BLOCKS

CACTUS FLOWER BLOCK WITH VALUES REVERSED

CACTUS FLOWER BLOCK

Sunrise

Directions:

1. Cut a light and dark 2⅛" strip and sew them together lengthwise. Cut 3¾" triangles from this set of strips. Cut off a ¼" strip from the bottom of each of these stripped triangles. (You will get both light and dark-based triangles from this set of strips. Choose one kind, and set the other kind aside for a different quilt, or make some blocks in this quilt using the other kind of triangles. *Please see note about stripped triangles on pg. 13.*)

3. Use a center* triangle, three dark, two medium, one light triangle, and two light-based stripped triangles, to make one wedge. Make six of these.

4. Sew the wedges three and three and sew across the middle to complete the hexagon block.

2. Cut for one block:

1.	6	center*	3½"	triangle
2.	24	dark	3½"	triangle
3.	6	light	3½"	triangle
4.	12	medium	3½"	triangle

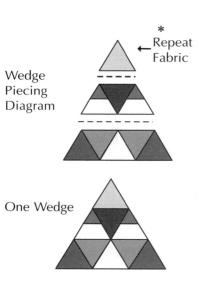

Wedge Piecing Diagram

* ← Repeat Fabric

One Wedge

Sunrise Block

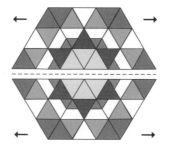

Piecing Diagram

Press seams away from center

Pinch and pin center

MOONSCAPE

Directions:

1. Cut a light and dark 2⅛" strip and sew them together lengthwise. Cut 3¾" triangles from this set of strips. Cut off a ¼" strip from the bottom of each of these stripped triangles. (You will get both light and dark-based triangles from this set of strips. Choose one kind, and set the other kind aside for a different quilt, or make some blocks in this quilt using the other kind of triangles. *Please see note about stripped triangles on pg. 13.*)

3. 3. Use a center* triangle, a dark triangle, two dark-tipped stripped triangles, and a flat pyramid to make one wedge. Make six of these.

4. Sew the wedges three and three and sew across the middle to complete the hexagon block.

3½" TRIANGLE CENTER REPEAT* FABRIC
All cutting is based on the 3½" triangle size.

2. Cut for one block:

1.	6	center*	3½"	triangle
2.	6	dark	3½"	triangle
3.	6	medium	9"	flat pyramid from 3¼" strip

Wedge Piecing Diagram

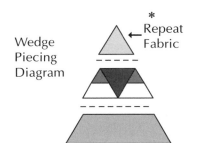

← Repeat Fabric

One Wedge

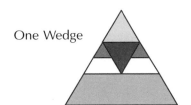

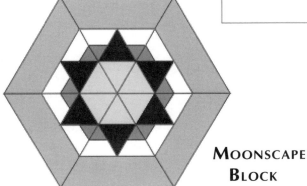

MOONSCAPE BLOCK

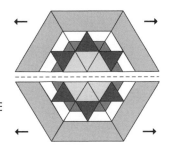

← →

← →

PIECING DIAGRAM
Press seams away from center
Pinch and pin center

CANDLE

1. Cut for one block:

1.	6	dark	1⅞"	diamond
2.	12	light	2⅛"	triangle
3.	6	center*	3½"	triangle
4.	6	medium	3¼"	long diamond
5.	6	med(reverse)	4⅝"	from a 1⅞" strip
6.	12	light	4⅞"	triangle

All cutting is based on the 3½" triangle size.

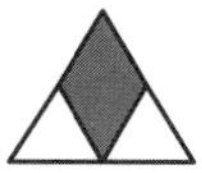

Directions:

2. Assemble a pieced triangle from a dark 1⅞" diamond and two light 2⅛" triangles. Sew on the 3½" long diamond, then the 4⅝" long diamond as shown. Then add the center* triangle and two light 4⅝" triangles as shown to make one wedge. Make six of these.

3. Sew the wedges three and three and sew across the middle to complete the hexagon block.

Pieced Triangle

Add Long Diamond

Add Second Long Diamond

One Wedge

CANDLE BLOCK

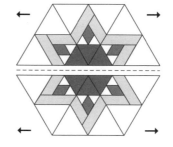

PIECING DIAGRAM

Press seams away from center

Pinch and pin center

FROZEN ROSES

All cutting is based on the 3½" triangle size.

Directions:

2. Sew one center diamond and two medium triangles into a pieced triangle as shown. Press to the triangles. Sew two floral diamonds and one solid triangle into a pieced strip as shown. Position the floral designs carefully. Press to the diamonds.

3. Pinch and pin and sew the pieced strip to the pieced triangle to make one wedge. Make 6. Press the crosswise seam to the center on three wedges and to the bottom on the other three wedges. Sew the wedges three and three and sew across the middle to make a hexagon block.

1. Cut for one block:

1.	6	center*	3¼"	diamonds
2.	12	medium	3½"	triangles
3.	6	dark	3½"	triangles
4.	12	light	3¼"	diamonds

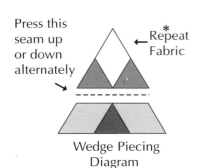

Press this seam up or down alternately

← Repeat Fabric*

Wedge Piecing Diagram

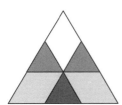

One Wedge

FROZEN ROSES BLOCK

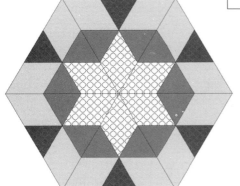

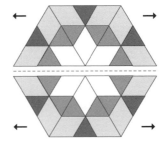

PIECING DIAGRAM
Press seams away from center
Pinch and pin center

FEATHER

1. Cut one each 2⅛" dark and light strips and sew right sides together with a ¼" seam down each side. Cut triangles from this set of strips. Pull apart at the tip and press open (sandwich-pieced triangles). You will need 24 for one block.

Pieced Strip

Directions:

3. Sew two sandwich-pieced triangles together with one dark 2⅛" triangle into a pieced strip as shown above. Make 12 of these.

4. Sew one of each long diamond onto the center diamond. Sew the pieced strips onto a medium triangle as shown. Add onto center diamond to complete one wedge. Make six.

5. Sew the wedges together into two sets of three. Pinch and pin and sew all the way across to join the two halves and complete the hexagon block.

Wedge Piecing Diagram

* ← Repeat Fabric

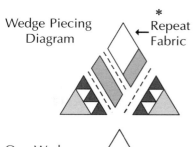

One Wedge

FEATHER BLOCK

2. Then cut for one block:

1.	6	center*	3¼"	diamond
2.	6	medium	3¼"	long diamond
3.	6	med(reverse)	4⅝"	from 1⅞" strip
4.	12	dark	2⅛"	triangle
5.	12	medium	3½"	triangle

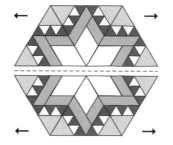

PIECING DIAGRAM
Press seams away from center
Pinch and pin center

36

BRILLIANT SKY

1. Cut for one block:

1.	6	center*	3¼"	diamond
2.	12	light	1⅞"	diamond
3.	24	dark	2⅛"	triangle
4.	12	light	3½"	triangle
5.	18	dark	3½"	triangle

3¼" DIAMOND CENTER REPEAT* FABRIC
All cutting is based on the 3½" triangle size.

Directions:

2. Sew one 1⅞" diamond and two 2⅛" triangles into a pieced triangle as shown. Make two of these. Sew one on each side of a center diamond. Assemble a strip as shown from three dark and two light 3½" triangles. Sew onto the pieced triangle from #2 above to make one wedge. Make six of these.

3. Sew the wedges three and three and sew across the middle to complete the hexagon block.

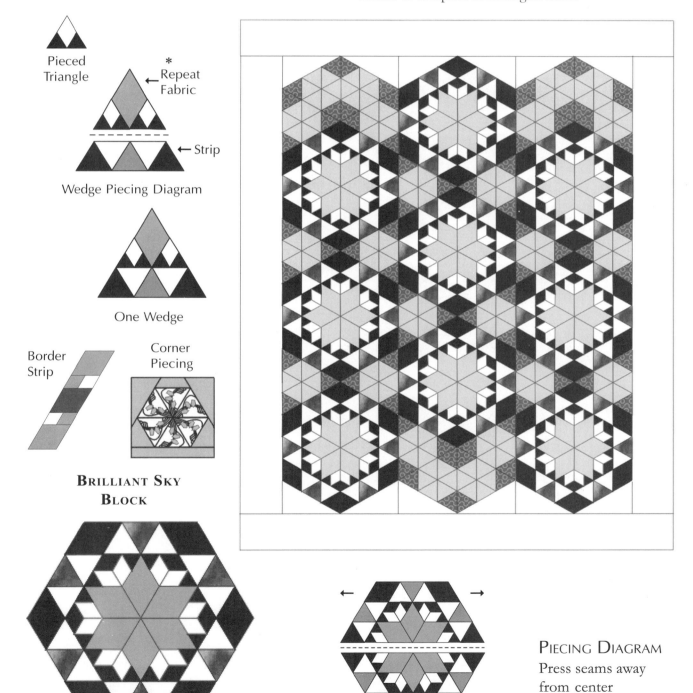

Pieced Triangle

* Repeat Fabric

← Strip

Wedge Piecing Diagram

One Wedge

Border Strip

Corner Piecing

BRILLIANT SKY BLOCK

PIECING DIAGRAM
Press seams away from center
Pinch and pin center

ICE CRYSTAL

1. Cut for one block:

1.	6	center*	3¼"	diamond
2.	12	light	1⅞"	diamond
3.	6	dark	1⅞"	diamond
4.	12	sets	2⅛"	matching triangles
5.	12	light	4⅞"	triangle

Directions:

2. Use a center diamond, two light 1⅞" diamonds, a dark 1⅞" diamond, two matching triangles, and two 4⅞" triangles to make one wedge. Make six of these.

3. Sew the wedges three and three and sew across the middle to complete the hexagon block.

All cutting is based on the 3½" triangle size.

Short Strip

Long Strip

← Repeat Fabric

Wedge Piecing Diagram

One Wedge

ICE CRYSTAL BLOCK

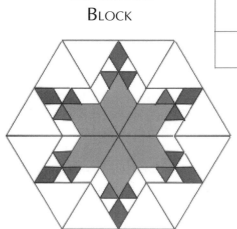

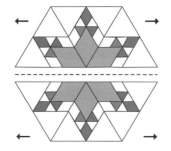

PIECING DIAGRAM
Press seams away from center
Pinch and pin center

FERN

1. Cut for one block:

1.	6	center*	3¼"	diamond
2.	30	sets	2⅛"	matching triangles
3.	12	light	4⅞"	triangle

Directions:

2. Make one selvage-to-selvage strip set of matching triangles for each block. Press to the light. Use a center diamond, five matching triangles, and two 4⅞" triangles to make one wedge. Make six of these.

3. Sew the wedges three and three and sew across the middle to complete the hexagon block.

All cutting is based on the 3½" triangle size.

Short Strip

Long Strip

*
Repeat Fabric

Wedge Piecing Diagram

One Wedge

FERN BLOCK

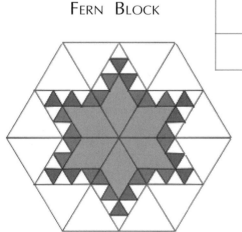

SOUTHERN COMFORT QUILT

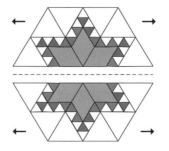

PIECING DIAGRAM
Press seams away from center
Pinch and pin center

BOTANICAL

All cutting is based on the 3½" triangle size.

1. Cut for one block:

1.	6	center*	3¼"	diamond
2.	24	light	2⅛"	triangles
3.	6	sets	2⅛"	matching triangles
4.	12	dark	1⅞"	diamond

Directions:

2. Cut a 4⅞" medium strip and two 1⅞" light strips and sew together lengthwise with the wider strip in the middle. Cut 4⅞" triangles from this set of strips. (**Or:** cut 12 light 4⅞" triangles as in Fern, pg. 39.) Use a center diamond, one matching triangle, two dark diamonds, four light 2⅛" triangles and two stripped 4⅞" triangles to make one wedge. Make six of these.

3. Sew the wedges three and three and sew across the middle to complete the hexagon block.

Diamond Strip And Reverse

* ← Repeat Fabric

Wedge Piecing Diagram

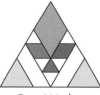

One Wedge

BOTANICAL BLOCK

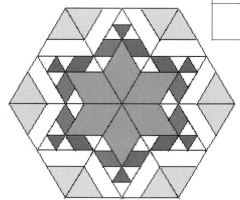

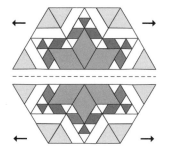

PIECING DIAGRAM
Press seams away from center
Pinch and pin center

SILK STOCKING

1. Cut for one block:

1.	6	center*	3¼"	diamond
2.	12	light	2⅛"	triangles
3.	6	dark	1⅞"	diamond
4.	6	dark	3½"	flat pyramid cut from 1⅞" strip

3¼" DIAMOND CENTER REPEAT* FABRIC
All cutting is based on the 3½" triangle size.

Directions:

2. Cut a 4⅞" medium strip and two 1⅞" light strips and sew together lengthwise with the wider strip in the middle. Cut 4⅞" triangles from this set of strips. (**Or:** cut 12 light 4⅞" triangles as in Fern, pg. 39.) Use a center diamond, one dark diamond, two light 2⅛" triangles, two flat pyramids, and two stripped 4⅞" triangles to make one wedge. Make six of these.

3. Sew the wedges three and three and sew across the middle to complete the hexagon block.

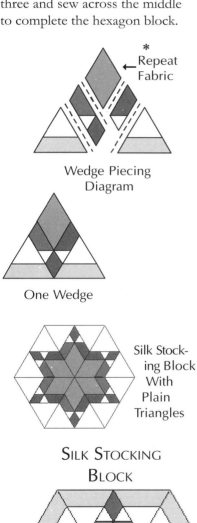

← * Repeat Fabric

Wedge Piecing Diagram

One Wedge

Silk Stocking Block With Plain Triangles

SILK STOCKING BLOCK

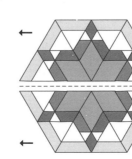

PIECING DIAGRAM
Press seams away from center
Pinch and pin center

TORCH

1. Cut for one block:

1.	6	center*	3¼"	diamond
2.	6	dark	1⅞"	diamond
3.	6	light	3¼"	long diamond and
4.	6	light	3¼"	reverse long diamond cut from 1⅞" strip

3¼" DIAMOND CENTER REPEAT* FABRIC
All cutting is based on the 3½" triangle size.

Directions:
2. Cut a 4⅞" medium strip and two 1⅞" light strips and sew together lengthwise with the wider strip in the middle. Cut 4⅞" triangles from this set of strips. (**Or:** cut 12 light 4⅞" triangles as in Fern, pg. 39.) Use a center diamond, one dark 1⅞" diamond, a long diamond and a reverse long diamond, and two stripped 4⅞" triangles to make one wedge. Make six of these.

3. Sew the wedges three and three and sew across the middle to complete the hexagon block.

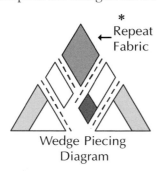

* ← **Repeat Fabric**

Wedge Piecing Diagram

One Wedge

Torch Block With Plain Triangles

TORCH BLOCK

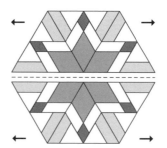

PIECING DIAGRAM
Press seams away from center
Pinch and pin center

Nested Hearts

1. Cut for one block:

1.	6	center*	3¼"	diamond
2.	12	dark	3¼"	gem shapes
3.	12	light	2⅛"	triangle
4.	6 light, 12 med.		3½"	triangle

All cutting is based on the 3½" triangle size.

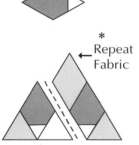

Pieced Diamond

*
← Repeat Fabric

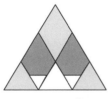

Wedge Piecing Diagram

One Wedge

Nested Hearts Block

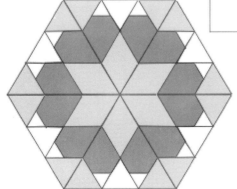

Directions:

2. Make a gem shape by cutting 1⅝" triangle off one end of a 3¼" diamond. Sew on a light 2⅛" triangle to make a pieced diamond. Make two. Assemble this with a center diamond, and one light and two medium 3½" triangles to make one wedge. Make six of these.

3. Sew the wedges three and three and sew across the middle to complete the hexagon block.

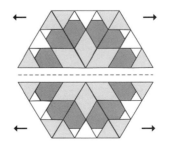

Piecing Diagram

Press seams away from center

Pinch and pin center

43

Popcorn

1. Cut for one block:

1.	6	center*	3¼"	gem
2.	6	light	2⅛"	triangle
3.	12	light	3½"	triangle
4.	12	medium	3½"	triangle
5.	6	dark	6¼"	flat pyramid from 3¼" strip

All cutting is based on the 3½" triangle size.

Pieced Diamond

* ← Repeat Fabric

Wedge Piecing Diagram

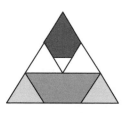

One Wedge

POPCORN BLOCK

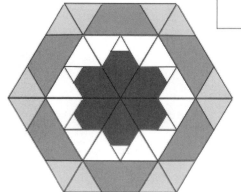

3¼" DIAMOND CENTER REPEAT* FABRIC

Directions:

2. Make a center* gem shape by cutting 1⅝" off one end of a 3¼" diamond. Sew on a light 2⅛" triangle to complete the pieced diamond. Add two light and two medium 3½" triangles and a dark 6¼" flat pyramid to make one wedge. Make six of these.

3. Sew the wedges three and three and sew across the middle to complete the hexagon block.

VINYARD QUILT

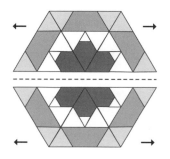

PIECING DIAGRAM
Press seams away from center
Pinch and pin center

WINGS OF A DOVE

1. Cut for one block:

1.	6	center*	3¼"	diamond
2.	12	light	3¼"	diamond
3.	18	dark	3½"	triangle

Directions:

2. Use a center diamond, two light diamonds, and three dark triangles to make one wedge as shown. Make six of these.

3. Sew the wedges three and three and sew across the middle to complete the hexagon block.

All cutting is based on the 3½" triangle size.

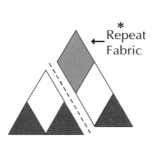

* ← Repeat Fabric

Wedge Piecing Diagram

One Wedge

WINGS OF A DOVE BLOCK

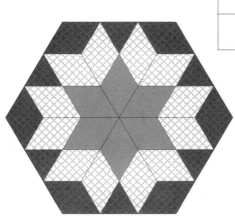

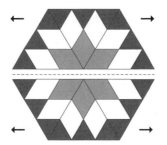

PIECING DIAGRAM
Press seams away from center
Pinch and pin center

EXPANDING STAR

All cutting is based on the 3½" triangle size.

Directions:

1. Cut a light and a dark 2⅛" strip and sew them together lengthwise. Cut 3¾" triangles from this set of strips. Cut off a ¼" strip from the bottom of each of these stripped triangles. (You will get both light and dark-based triangles from this set of strips. Choose one kind, and set the other kind aside for a different quilt, or make some blocks in this quilt using the other kind of triangles. *Please see note about stripped triangles on pg. 13.*)

2. In addition, cut for one block:

1.	6	center*	3¼"	diamond
2.	6	medium	3½"	triangle
3.	12	dark	4⅞"	flat pyramid (from 3¼" strip)

3. Use two stripped triangles, a center diamond, two flat pyramids, and one medium triangle to complete one wedge. Make six of these.

4. Sew the wedges together into two sets of three. Pinch and pin and sew all the way across to join the two halves and complete the hexagon block.

Wedge Piecing Diagram

*← Repeat Fabric

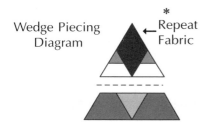

One Wedge

EXPANDING STAR BLOCK

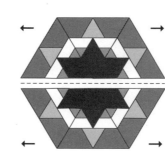

PIECING DIAGRAM
Press seams away from center
Pinch and pin center

EXPANDING STAR VARIATION

Instead of: *(as on previous page)*

3.	12	dark	4⅞"	flat pyramid (from 3¼" strip)

Directions: 1. Substitute (as shown):

3.	12	medium	3½"	triangle
4.	6	dark	3¼"	long diamond (from 1⅞" strip)
5.	6	dark (reverse)	3¼"	long diamond (from 1⅞" strip)

All cutting is based on the 3½" triangle size.

Pieced Flat Pyramid
And Reverse

2. Sew the long diamonds or the reverse long diamonds to the left or right of the medium triangle to make pieced flat pyramids and their reverse. Make one of each. Assemble as on pg. 00, substituting pieced flat pyramids. In this design, the center of the setting triangles must be made from three dark and three light 3½" triangles, alternating values. Then line up the dark triangle at the side of each block.

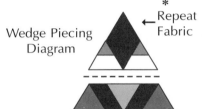

Wedge Piecing
Diagram

← Repeat *
Fabric

One Wedge

EXPANDING STAR BLOCK VARIATION

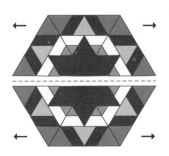

PIECING DIAGRAM
Press seams away
from center
Pinch and pin center

SHERIFF'S STAR

1. Cut for one block:

1.	6	center*	3¼"	diamond
2.	24	dark	3½"	triangle
3.	6	medium	6¼"	flat pyramid
				from 3¼" strip

Directions:

2. Assemble a center diamond, four dark triangles, and one flat pyramid to make one wedge. Make six of these.

3. Sew the wedges three and three and sew across the middle to complete the hexagon block.

All cutting is based on the 3½" triangle size.

* ← Repeat Fabric

Wedge Piecing Diagram

One Wedge

SHERIFF'S STAR BLOCK

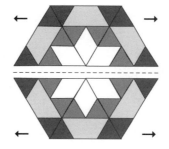

PIECING DIAGRAM
Press seams away from center
Pinch and pin center

Seashells (above), 61" x 76½". Stacked china teapots look like parts of seashells found on a beach. A second repeat fabric, a kitchen print of flowers and cherries on light yellow, carries the design out to the second level of the block. Pieced by Sara Nephew and machine quilted by Judy Irish.

Fruit Salad (above right), 48" x 54". Judy cleverly displays her repeat fabric in the borders of her quilt. Three blocks of BIGFOOT, plus setting triangles and borders, makes a picture that looks good enough to eat. Fancy food! A curvy stripe in black and white adds a ripple effect. The stacked repeat fabric is by Alexander Henry Textiles. Pieced and machine quilted by Judy Irish.

Cinco de Mayo (right), 60" x 76½", explodes with hot color against a starry sky. The sharp points of the TEXAS SUNFLOWER block strike sparks from the spinning folk-art motifs created by peeled and sliced apples. Pieced by Sara Nephew and machine quilted by Judy Irish.

Mango Madness (above), 59½" x 68", glows with the beauty of a stained glass "rose window" in a cathedral. Though the fabric patterns themselves are wildly active, Terri's firmly consistent color placement emphasizes the GULL block structure and the secondary designs it forms. Pieced by Terri Shinn and machine quilted by Judy Irish.

Tropical Roses (above), 61" x 78½". This is the second Serendipity quilt made by the author. The three versions of the FROZEN ROSES design shown on these two pages demonstrate the many variations possible with just one block design. Choice of repeat fabric changes everything. Pieced by Sara Nephew and machine quilted by Judy Irish.

Spring Rose Garden (right), 52½" x 61½". Substituting light for dark in the FROZEN ROSES block reveals the six-pointed stars formed by the setting triangles between the blocks. Decorator fabric and pastel accent colors were a good choice for a floating breezy look. The minimal border makes a smaller quilt out of eight blocks. Pieced and machine quilted by Joan Hanson.

Frozen Roses, 75½" x 95½", was the first Serendipity quilt pieced by the author. The author kept running out of fabric and hitting another quilt shop. Exhilarated by the possibilities, Sara used repeats in every possible place, resulting in an extremely rich look. Texture and design detail meet the eye with every glance. All four repeat fabrics are of roses on a light background, so color, value, and theme pull the quilt together. Sixteen blocks make a quilt big enough to use crosswise on a queen-sized bed. Hand-quilted by Ardell Gillespie.

Desert Flowers Dream Of Water (above), 45" x 41". Two blocks of CACTUS FLOWER combine with buttons and other stacked fabrics for an elegant little wall hanging. This quilt cleverly shows a cactus plant with buds and two huge blooms. Desert heat reflects and repeats in orange and red accents throughout the masterfully controlled design. The narrow inner border is part of that fire. Pieced and machine quilted by Eda Lee Haas.

Festival, (above) 58½" x 75". The SUNRISE block creates a strong frame for classic stars, and a sophisticated color palette complements Asian-inspired fabrics. Dark background fabric sets off each individual block and setting triangle while creating a secondary design of its own. Pieced by Kathleen Malarky and machine quilted by Judy Irish.

Marguerita, (right) 59" x 65". Fruit and flowers in hot colors. The large center diamonds of the FIN block allow the stacked repeat fabric full scope to take over this design. During a Pacific Northwest winter, this quilt radiates the heat of Florida, California, all the southern states. All material by Andover Fabrics. Pieced by Sara Nephew and machine quilted by Judy Irish.

October Country, 60" x 66". A little bit of purple adds incandescence to the designs created by these kaleides-coping stars. Who would believe autumn leaves could be so beautiful? Pam's sharp-edged border combines the pieced triangle units used in the star points with stripped triangles from the outside corners of the blocks. More stripped triangles inserted into the setting triangles at four corners repeat the double diamond motif and add balance to the quilt. The featured block is SPARKLING SKY. Pieced and machine quilted by Pam Pifer.

Expanding Star, (right) 67" x 85".
Metallic gold details and beige marble-like setting fabric add an architectural flavor to this unique quilt. Using the same dark fabric for the corners of the blocks and the corners of the setting triangles drops out the background and focuses attention on all the marvelous floral patterns in the stacked repeats. Pieced by Kathleen Springer and machine quilted by Marianne Roan.

Blooming (below left), 57" x 80".
A seemingly relaxed mix of background fabrics adds variety and interest to this design. This asymmetrical arrangement is in the spirit of the East, complementing the Asian-inspired fabric used in the stars and small hexagons. An unusual plan for the borders complements the carefully balanced quilt. Pieced by Nadi Lane and machine quilted by Karen Ebbesmeyer.

Red Snowfall, (below) 55" x 72". The soft motifs in the centers of the blocks and setting triangles are pretty, but the red stripes on the corners of every BIG TRIANGLE block steal the show; whirling, weaving, glowing like jewels. Pieced by Janet Goad and machine quilted by Judy Irish.

54

Happy Domesticity, 69½" x 82½". This time Virginia did not stack her fabric, but instead cut the whole quilt one piece at a time (fussy-cutting). Her concern was to do her best to make all the little stripes match perfectly, which they do. This kitchen-inspired print in the HEARTS block creates designs that are definitely fun to look at. Narrow, wide, and pieced borders are added to frame the wonderful quilt top she produced. Pieced and machine quilted by Virginia Anderson.

Brilliant Sky (above), 62" x 80". The dark background of the focus print adds depth and dimension to this exciting quilt. A playfully controlled approach to color and value placement keeps the eye moving, enjoying the richness of detail. Joan's pieced border is not extremely complicated, but dresses up the whole design. This quilt received Best-Of-Show (Viewer's Choice) at the Quilter's Anonymous 2003 Quilt Show. Pieced by Joan Dawson and machine quilted by Judy Irish.

Spiral Passions (facing page top left), 43" x 54", is a small wall hanging with a lot of visual interest. The light green around the outer edge of the PINWHEEL blocks fades into the background leaving ornamented balls and stars like a floating dream of a Christmas tree. Pieced by Joanne File and machine quilted by Judy Irish.

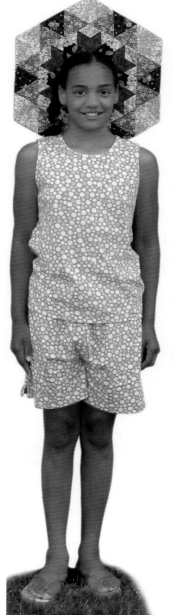

In the summer of 2002 our two granddaughters, Taylor and Ashley, spent every day at our house. One day I was taking a snapshot of Joan Dawson's Brilliant Sky quilt. It was pinned on the outside wall of our house and Taylor, then ten years old, jumped in front of the quilt top and said, "Grandma, take my picture!" By <u>happy accident</u> Taylor was exactly the right height and put herself perfectly in the center of the quilt, so she ended up with a pieced halo. This is an excellent example of serendipity.

Japanese Garden (above right), 62" x 80". Joan had a big pile of beautiful hexagons made from 5" triangles. When the author started producing designs for this book, Joan phoned and said, "Make me a design to use these hexagons!" SIMPLE CROCHET was the result, and the beginning (thanks to Joan) of a whole new group of blocks with larger center pieces. Such designs need to be handled carefully, but she has done an excellent job with these deceptively simple-looking blocks. Pieced and machine quilted by Joan Dawson.

Wings Of A Dove (right), 65½" x 82½". Delicate pastels combine in a song to spring flowers. Colors scattered seemingly at random in the blocks and setting triangles are soft and appealing, making this quilt easy to live with and enjoy. Pieced by Kathy Kryla and machine quilted by Judy Irish.

Fleur et Feuillage, 68½" x 81½". Virginia used stacked repeats in this quilt and really felt a sense of freedom as she cut six pieces at once. We know she is willing to take the time to make a beautiful quilt, just by looking at the two examples of her work in this book. In this amazing quilt, a sprightly leaf fabric is also stacked and used as the corners of the setting triangles and in the border. Taken all together, her fabric, texture, and color choices and her careful cutting make a precise, formal design that is rich in color, detail, and meaning. Pieced and machine quilted by Virginia Anderson.

Southern Comfort (left), 60½" x 78". After using a variety of accent colors it seemed this quilt needed more organization. Arranging the background into three vertical rows of color pulled all the parts of the design together. The FERN block makes a beautiful feathered star. Sewn exclusively from In The Beginning fabrics, which in this quilt work together for a soft delicate effect. Pieced by Sara Nephew and machine quilted by Judy Irish.

Butterfly Prayers (below right), 64" x 80". Butterflies on black twirl themselves into tight designs like filigree jewelry. Accent colors were chosen based on details in the butterflies. And the blocks were built one at a time trying all possible variations in color and value. A friend remarked that the design looked "kind of churchy." Thus the name of the quilt. The block is LOG PETAL. Pieced by Sara Nephew and machine quilted by Judy Irish.

Not Your Typical Hawaiian Quilt (below), 58" x 66". Scott is never afraid to mix fabrics. A quantity of prints of different scale makes the design richer and more interesting. The focus print is Hawaiian shirts against a sky-colored background. The FISH block is a good choice for a Hawaii-themed fabric collection. Pieced by Scott Hansen, machine quilted by Judy Irish.

Valentine Lace, 79" x 95". These wildflowers make marvelously varied bouquets, wreaths, and floral medallions. Another intricate design is introduced in the fussy-cut diamonds radiating from the center of each THIMBLE STAR block. The author had only one yard of this fleur-de-lis fabric. At the beginning, she tore the fabric in half lengthwise to make it easier to handle, as is done when stacking repeats. Unfortunately, this meant 13 diamonds had to be pieced back together in the end. The floral fabric also ran out, so nine little stars were made from fussy-cut diamonds to substitute in the setting triangles. Pieced by Sara Nephew and machine quilted by Judy Irish.

Sweet William, 64" x 81". Huge flowers produce a perturbation of petals. Hot reds, pinks, and oranges are cooled by blues in the background and border. The TRIM block has large center pieces that give importance to the floral fabric. All fabric from The Ehrlanger Group/Woodrow Studios. Pieced by Sara Nephew and machine quilted by Judy Irish.

Sherbet Fizz, (above) 58½" x 76". The glowing accent colors of this quilt; red and green, orange and purple, add light and life to an already luminescent focus fabric. The narrow inner border reflects the light from this fire. What a transformation for a plain block like SHERIFF'S STAR! Pieced by Diane Coombs and machine quilted by Judy Irish.

Hiram's Valentine Circa 1933, (right) 40" x 51". Five FEATHER blocks make an exciting new arrangement when turned on point. Scott carefully placed fabric to extend the block backgrounds and make diamonds of different colors behind the feathered stars, a sharp secondary design that adds diagonal motion to the mixed colors and textures of another great scrappy look. These 30's-inspired motifs created, when stacked, an amazing variety of patterns to enjoy. Pieced by Scott Hansen and machine quilted by Judy Irish.

Dark Feather (above left), 63" x 80½". George put so much color emphasis on the twinkling triangles playing around each star that at first we don't notice the beautiful kaleidoscopes in the center of each star and setting triangle. The pink and dark green triangles sparkle and move as we look at them, and hot pink is mirrored again in the pinstripe inner border. This quilt is full of surprises! Pieced and machine quilted by George Taylor.

Starlight, Star Bright (above right), 56" x 78", looks quiet and secret and shadowy, like snow falling at midnight. There's something restful about these color choices. Janet had room for ten blocks, but chose to use more setting triangles instead. Anything goes! Pieced by Janet Goad and machine quilted by Linda Daughtetee.

Serendipity Stars (bottom facing page), 61" x 58½". Carole asked for this EXPANDING STAR VARIATION because she could see the design possiblities. To recreate this quilt you must work it out step-by-step, since the directions are not given. Hints: Assemble in vertical rows for easy piecing. Strips 3¼" wide can be sewn onto pieced units and trimmed to the correct angle. The large darker green flat pyramid in the inner border left and right should be cut from a 3¼" strip at 11¾" on the ruler. Pieced and machine quilted by Carole Rush.

Vinyard, (above) 67" x 76". Fussy-cut suns shine on this field of vines. Background pastels echo the light and shadow of sky and sun on leaves, and the suns imitate medals won by superior wines. The POPCORN block provides many opportunities to use repeats in different places for special effects. Happy accident allowed Sara to find fabric in her stash to make the fill-in corners and the viney border. The stacked repeat fabric of grapes and leaves is from Michael Miller Fabrics, Inc. Pieced by Sara Nephew and machine quilted by Judy Irish.

Dance Of The Snow Queen (right), 19¾" x 60½", Three of the FEATHER block with their setting hexagons make a striking center-piece for a happy family meal or a special holiday. Scott Hansen again shows off his ability to mix bright scraps for a strong design. Pieced by Scott Hansen and machine quilted by Judy Irish.

Balance (above), 63" x 80½", The play of bright and soft colors over the surface of this quilt is a strong pattern on which to place the lacy details of the stacked repeat kaleid-escopes. A deceptively simple looking visual experi-ence that gives pleasure wherever you look. Pieced and machine quilted by Pam Cope.

I Never Promised You A Rose Garden (right), 89" x 91", Diane used a soft stacked repeat in the center and another, a brighter print, in the six triangles filled with roses around the outer edge of the WEDGE STAR block. The mix of different sized textures and the color variations produce a rich, lush quilt. Pieced by Diane Coombs and machine quilted by Judy Irish.

SPARKLING SKY

Directions:

2. Sew 1⅞" diamond and two dark 2⅛" triangles into a pieced triangle as shown. Make two of these. Add a center diamond, a flat pyramid, and two dark 3½" triangles to make one wedge. Make six of these.

3. Sew the wedges together into two sets of three. Line up and pin the centers and sew all the way across to join the two halves and complete the hexagon block.

Pieced Triangle

Wedge Piecing Diagram

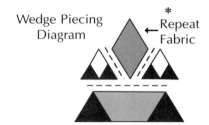

← Repeat Fabric *

One Wedge

SPARKLING SKY BLOCK

3¼" DIAMOND CENTER REPEAT* FABRIC

All cutting is based on the 3½" triangle size.

1. Cut for one block:

1.	6	center*	3¼"	diamond
2.	12	light	1⅞"	diamond
3.	24	dark	2⅛"	triangle
4.	6	medium	6¼"	flat pyramid from 3¼" strip
5.	12	dark	3½"	triangle

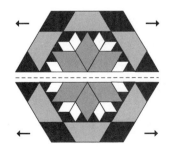

PIECING DIAGRAM
Press seams away from center
Pinch and pin center

Ribbon

1. Cut for one block:

1.	6	center*	3¼"	diamond
2.	6	light	3¼"	triangle
3.	6 ea.	dark/med.	6¼"	flat pyramid from 3¼" strip

3¼" DIAMOND CENTER REPEAT* FABRIC

All cutting is based on the 3½" triangle size.

Directions:

2. Use a center diamond, a medium pyramid, a dark pyramid, and one light triangle to make one wedge as shown. Make six of these.

3. Sew the wedges three and three and sew across the middle to complete the hexagon block.

Pieced Strip

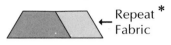

← Repeat * Fabric

Pieced Triangle

* Repeat Fabric →

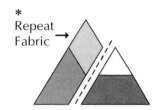

Wedge Piecing Diagram

One Wedge

RIBBON BLOCK

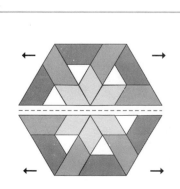

PIECING DIAGRAM
Press seams away from center
Pinch and pin center

BALANCE

1. Cut for one block:

1.	6	center*	3¼"	diamond
2.	12	light	3½"	flat pyramid
				from 1⅞" strip
3.	6	dark	3½"	triangle
4.	12	med	4⅞"	triangle

All cutting is based on the 3½" triangle size.

Directions:

2. Use a center diamond, two light 3½" flat pyramids, one dark triangle, and two light 4⅞" triangles to make one wedge as shown. Make six of these.

3. Sew the wedges three and three and sew across the middle to complete the hexagon block.

* ← Repeat Fabric

Wedge Piecing Diagram

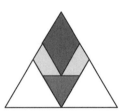

One Wedge

BALANCE BLOCK

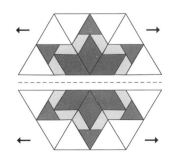

PIECING DIAGRAM
Press seams away from center
Pinch and pin center

BLOOMING

1. Cut for one block:

1.	6	center*	3¼"	diamond
2.	6	dark	3¼"	diamond
3.	12	light	3½"	triangle
4.	6	dark	6¼"	flat pyramid from 3¼" strip

Directions:

2. Use a center diamond, a dark diamond, a dark flat pyramid, and two light triangles to make one wedge as shown. Make six of these.

3. Sew the wedges three and three and sew across the middle to complete the hexagon block.

All cutting is based on the 3½" triangle size.

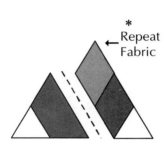

* ← Repeat Fabric

Wedge Piecing Diagram

One Wedge

BLOOMING BLOCK

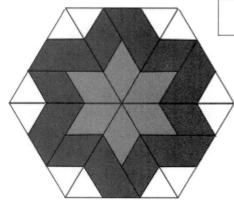

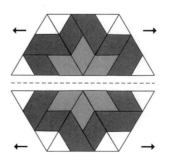

PIECING DIAGRAM
Press seams away from center
Pinch and pin center

PINWHEEL

1. Cut for one block:

1.	6 medium	3½"	triangle
2.	6 center* and 6 medium	6¼"	flat pyramid
			(3¼" strip)
3.	6 dark and 6 dark reverse	3¼"	long diamond
			(1⅞" strip)

All cutting is based on the 3½" triangle size.

Directions:

2. Sew triangle to 6¼" flat pyramid as shown. Add a medium flat pyramid, and a 3¼" long diamond and its reverse to make one wedge. Make six of these.

3. Sew the wedges together into two sets of three. Line up and pin the centers and sew all the way across to join the two halves and complete the hexagon block.

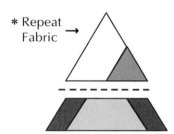

* Repeat Fabric →

Wedge Piecing Diagram

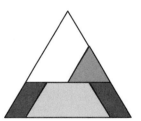

One Wedge

PINWHEEL BLOCK

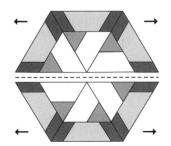

PIECING DIAGRAM
Press seams away from center
Pinch and pin center

ROSE PINWHEEL

6¼" FLAT PYRAMID CENTER REPEAT* FABRIC

Directions:

2. Sew triangle to 6¼" flat pyramid as shown. Add another 3½" triangle and two 4⅞" flat pyramids to make one wedge. Make six of these.

3. Sew the wedges together into two sets of three. Line up and pin the centers and sew all the way across to join the two halves and complete the hexagon block.

1. Cut for one block:

1.	6	center*	6¼"	flat pyramid
2.	12	dark	4⅞"	from 3¼" strip
3.	12	medium	3½"	triangle

All cutting is based on the 3½" triangle size.

Wedge Piecing Diagram

One Wedge

ROSE PINWHEEL BLOCK

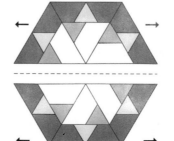

PIECING DIAGRAM
Press seams away from center
Pinch and pin center

BUDDING

1. Cut for one block:

1.	6	center*	4⅞"	triangle
2.	6	medium	4⅞"	triangle
3.	12	dark	3¼"	hexagon
(cut a 1⅝" triangle off each end of a 3¼"diamond)				
4.	36	light	2⅛"	triangle

All cutting is based on the 3½" triangle size.

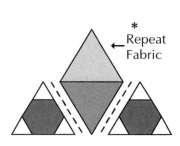

Wedge Piecing Diagram

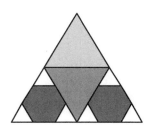

One Wedge

BUDDING BLOCK

Directions:

2. Sew three medium 2⅛" triangles onto separate sides of a hexagon as shown to make a pieced triangle. Make two of these.

3. Use two pieced triangles from #2 above, plus a center triangle and a medium triangle to make one wedge. Make six of these.

4. Sew the wedges three and three and sew across the middle to make a hexagon block.

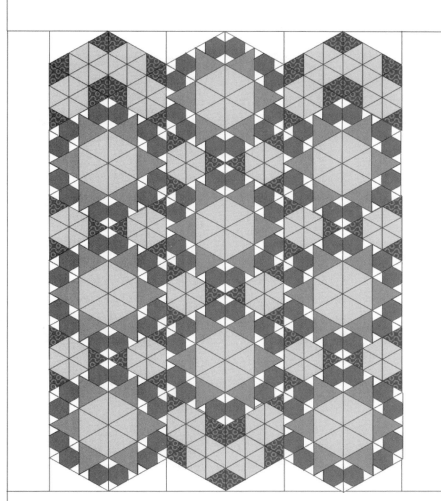

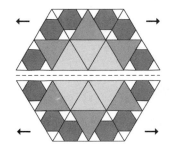

PIECING DIAGRAM
Press seams away from center
Pinch and pin center

71

FISH

1. Cut a light and dark 2⅛" strip and sew them together lengthwise. Cut 3¾" triangles from this set of strips. Cut off a ¼" strip from the bottom of each of these stripped triangles. You will get both light and dark-based triangles from this set of strips. *Please see the note about stripped triangles on pg. 13.*

2. Then cut for one block:

1.	6	center*	4⅞"	triangle
2.	12	dark	1⅞"	diamond
3.	6	light	2⅛"	triangle
4.	12	medium	4⅞"	flat pyramid from 1⅞" strip

Directions:

3. Sew two dark diamonds and one light triangle into a pieced strip as shown. Sew this strip on the bottom of a light-based stripped triangle(A). Sew the flat pyramids on the bottom of the dark-based stripped triangles(B) (Or log cabin on a 1⅞" strip and trim to a 4⅞" triangle).

Pieced Strip

4. Use one (A), two (B), and one center triangle to make one wedge. Make six of these. Sew the wedges together into two sets of three. Pinch and pin and sew all the way across to join the two halves and complete the hexagon block.

Wedge Piecing Diagram

← *Repeat Fabric*

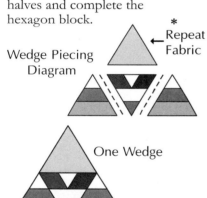

One Wedge

FISH BLOCK

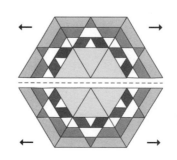

PIECING DIAGRAM
Press seams away from center
Pinch and pin center

72

GULL

1. Cut a light and dark 2⅛" strip and sew them together lengthwise. Cut 3¾" triangles from this set of strips. Cut off a ¼" strip from the bottom of each of these stripped triangles. (You will get both light and dark-based triangles from this set of strips. Choose one kind, and set the other aside for a different quilt, or make some blocks in this quilt using the other kind of triangles. *Please see note about stripped triangles on pg. 13.*)

2. Then cut for one block:

1.	6	center*	4⅞"	triangle
2.	6	light	2⅛"	triangle
3.	12	dark	3½"	flat pyramid (1⅞" strip)
4.	6 each	medium	3¼"	long diamond (1⅞" strip) and reverse long diamond

Directions:

3. Sew two dark flat pyramids and a 2⅛" triangle into a pieced strip as shown (A). Sew three stripped triangles into a flat pyramid (B).

Pieced Strip A

Flat Pyramid B

4. Use a center triangle, one (A), one (B), and a long diamond and its reverse to make one wedge. Make six.

* Repeat Fabric

Wedge Piecing Diagram

5. Sew the wedges three and three and sew across the middle to complete the hexagon block.

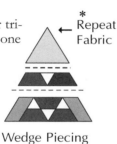
One Wedge

GULL BLOCK

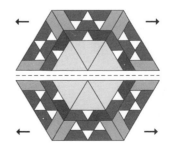

PIECING DIAGRAM
Press seams away from center
Pinch and pin center

HEARTS

1. Cut a light and dark 2⅛" strip and sew them together lengthwise. Cut 3¾" triangles from this set of strips. Cut off a ¼" strip from the bottom of each of these stripped triangles. (You will get both light and dark-based triangles from this set of strips. Choose one kind, and set the other kind aside for a different quilt, or make some blocks in this quilt using the other kind of triangles. *Please see note about stripped triangles on pg.13.*)

4⅞" TRIANGLE CENTER REPEAT* FABRIC
All cutting is based on the 3½" triangle size.

2. Cut for one block:

1.	6	center*	4⅞"	triangle
2.	6	light	2⅛"	triangle
3.	12	dark	3½"	flat pyramid (1⅞" strip)
4.	6	medium	6¼"	flat pyramid (3¼" strip)

Directions:

2. Use a center triangle, a light 2⅛" triangle, two dark flat pyramids, a medium flat pyramid, and two stripped triangles to make one wedge. Make six of these.

3. Sew the wedges together into two sets of three. Pinch and pin and sew all the way across to join the two halves and complete the hexagon block.

Wedge Piecing Diagram
→ *Repeat Fabric

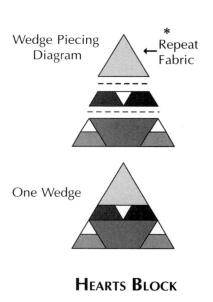

One Wedge

HEARTS BLOCK

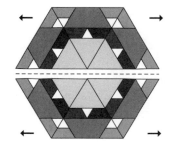

PIECING DIAGRAM
Press seams away from center
Pinch and pin center

SIMPLE CROCHET

1. Cut for one block:

1.	6	center*	4⅞"	triangle
2.	6	dark	4⅞"	triangle
3.	12	light	4⅞"	triangle

Directions:

2. Assemble a center triangle, two medium triangles, and one dark triangle to make one wedge. Make six of these.

3. Sew the wedges three and three and sew across the middle to complete the hexagon block.

All cutting is based on the 3½" triangle size.

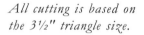

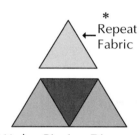

* ← Repeat Fabric

Wedge Piecing Diagram

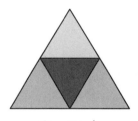

One Wedge

SIMPLE CROCHET BLOCK

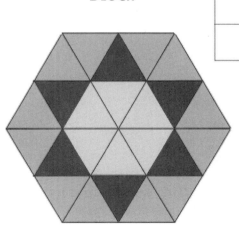

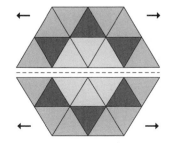

PIECING DIAGRAM
Press seams away from center
Pinch and pin center

DARK FEATHER

1. Cut one each 2⅛" dark and light strips and sew right sides together with a ¼" seam down each side. Cut 2⅛" triangles from this set of strips. Pull apart at the tip and press open (sandwich-pieced triangles). You will need 24 for one block.

2. Then cut for one block:

1.	6	center*	4⅝"	diamond
2.	18	dark	2⅛"	triangle
3.	12	light	2⅛"	triangle
4.	12	medium	3½"	triangle

Directions:

3. Sew two sandwich-pieced triangles together with one dark 2⅛" triangle into a pieced strip as shown. Make two of these.

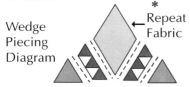

4. Sew both pieced strips onto the center* diamond. Add a medium triangle on each corner as shown to complete one wedge. Make six of these.

Wedge Piecing Diagram

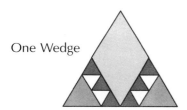

← *Repeat Fabric

5. Sew the wedges together into two sets of three. Pinch and pin and sew all the way across to join the two halves and complete the hexagon block.

One Wedge

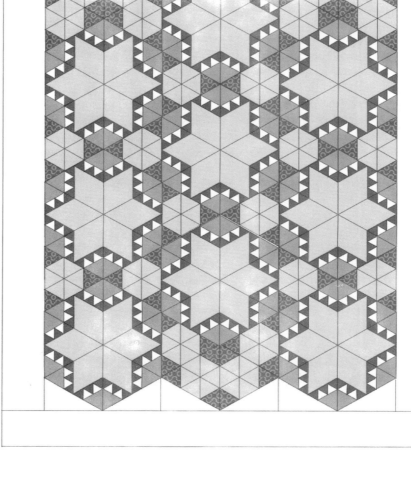

DARK FEATHER BLOCK

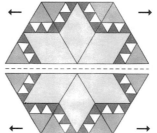

PIECING DIAGRAM
Press seams away from center
Pinch and pin center

ECHO FEATHER

1. Cut a light and dark 2⅛" strip and sew them together lengthwise. Cut 3¾" triangles from this set of strips. Cut off a ¼" strip from the bottom of each of these stripped triangles. (You will get both light and dark-based triangles from this set of strips. Choose one kind, and set the other kind aside for a different quilt, or make some blocks in this quilt using the other kind of triangles. *Please see note about stripped triangles on pg. 13.*)

2. Cut for one block:

1.	6	center*	4⅝"	diamond
2.	12	dark	2⅛"	triangle

3. Cut 2⅛" dark and light strips and sew right sides together with a ¼" seam down both sides. Cut triangles from this set of strips. Pull apart at the tip and press open (sandwich-pieced). You will need 24 for one block.

Directions:

4. Use two sandwich-pieced triangles and one dark 2⅛" triangle to make a pieced strip as shown. Make two of these. Add a center diamond and two stripped triangles to make one wedge. Make six of these. Sew the wedges three and three and sew across the middle to finish the block.

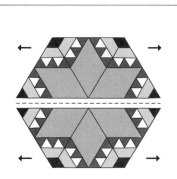

Pieced Strip

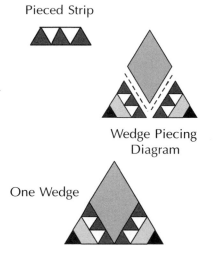

Wedge Piecing Diagram

One Wedge

ECHO FEATHER BLOCK

PIECING DIAGRAM
Press seams away from center
Pinch and pin center

LOTUS FLOWER

1. Cut for one block:

1.	6	center*	4⅝"	diamond
2.	6	light	2¾"	triangle

Directions:

2. Cut a 2¼" triangle off one end of the center diamond (do the stack of six diamonds all at once) and sew on the 2¾" triangle to make one pieced gem shape as shown. Make six of these.

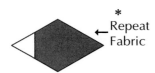

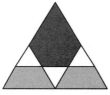

Pieced Gem Shape

Sew from the outside in

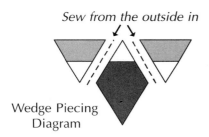

Wedge Piecing Diagram

One Wedge

LOTUS FLOWER BLOCK

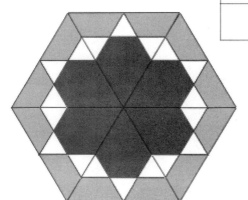

3. Cut a light and a medium 2⅞" strip and sew them together lengthwise. Press to the light. Cut 5¼" triangles from this set of strips. Set aside the light-based triangles for another project. Trim ⅜" from the bottom of all the dark-based pieced triangles. Sew two pieced triangles to a gem shape to make one wedge. (Sew from the outside in.) Make six of these.

4. Sew the wedges three and three and sew across the middle to complete the hexagon block.

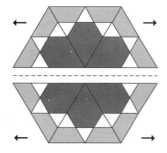

PIECING DIAGRAM
Press seams away from center
Pinch and pin center

DANCING LOTUS

VARIATIONS

DANCING LOTUS BLOCK

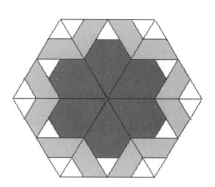

One Wedge

Wedge Piecing Diagram

A quilter could decide to use the light-based stripped triangles instead, which would change the look of the design. Or... Simply turning the stripped triangle into the two other possible positions produces two more block designs, Radiant Lotus (at right) and Dancing Lotus above. There are other blocks in this book using stripped triangles that could be turned..

RADIANT LOTUS

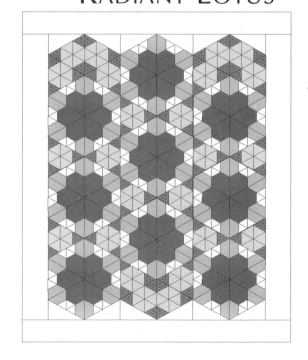

RADIANT LOTUS BLOCK

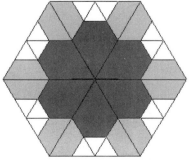

FIN

1. Cut for one block:

1.	6	center*	4⅝"	diamond
2.	12	light	3½"	flat pyramid from 1⅞" strip
3.	24	dark	2⅛"	triangle
4.	12	medium	3½"	triangle

Directions:

2. Use a light flat pyramid and two dark 2⅛" triangles to make a pieced strip as shown. Make two of these. Add a center diamond and two medium triangles to make one wedge. Make six of these.

3. Sew the wedges three and three and sew across the middle to complete the hexagon block.

All cutting is based on the 3½" triangle size.

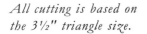

Pieced Strip

* Repeat Fabric →

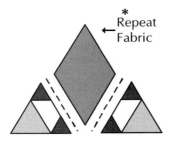

Wedge Piecing Diagram

One Wedge

FIN BLOCK

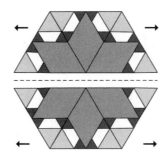

PIECING DIAGRAM
Press seams away from center
Pinch and pin center

80

BIG STAR

1. Cut for one block:

1.	6	center*	4⅝"	diamond
2.	12	medium	4⅞"	triangle

Directions:

2. Sew two triangles to a diamond to make one wedge. Make six of these.

3. Sew the wedges together into two sets of three. Pinch and pin and sew all the way across to join the two halves and complete the hexagon block.

All cutting is based on the 3½" triangle size.

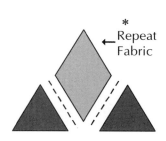

Repeat Fabric

Wedge Piecing Diagram

One Wedge

BIG STAR BLOCK

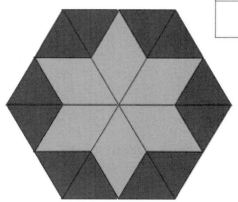

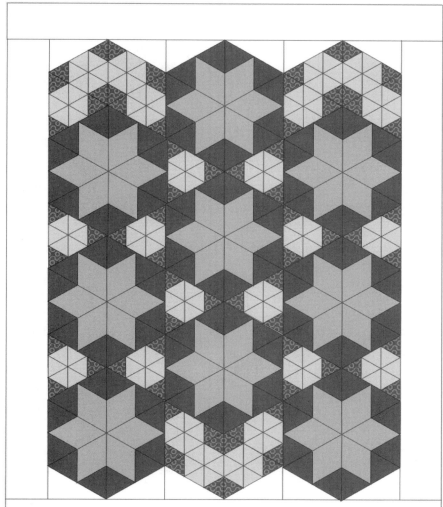

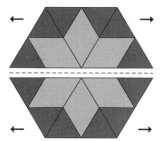

PIECING DIAGRAM
Press seams away from center
Pinch and pin center

PETAL

All cutting is based on the 3½" triangle size.

1. Cut for one block:

1.	6	center*	6¼"	triangle
2.	6	dark	6¼"	flat pyramid (from 3¼" strip)
3.	12	light	3½"	triangle

Directions:

2. Assemble as shown to make one wedge. Make six of these.

3. Sew the wedges three and three and sew across the middle to complete the hexagon block.

Pieced Strip

*
← Repeat
Fabric

Wedge Piecing
Diagram

One Wedge

PETAL BLOCK

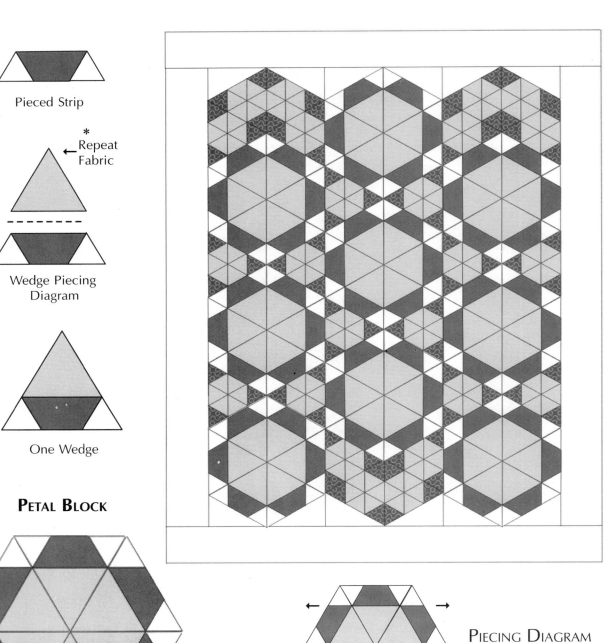

PIECING DIAGRAM
Press seams away
from center
Pinch and pin center

TOOTH

1. Cut for one block:

1.	6	center*	6¼"	triangle
2.	12	light	3½"	triangle
3.	18	dark	3½"	triangle

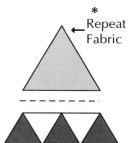

Pieced Strip

* ← Repeat Fabric

Wedge Piecing Diagram

One Wedge

TOOTH BLOCK

6¼" TRIANGLE CENTER REPEAT* FABRIC
All cutting is based on the 3½" triangle size.

Directions:

2. Assemble as shown to make one wedge. Make six of these.

3. Sew the wedges three and three and sew across the middle to complete the hexagon block.

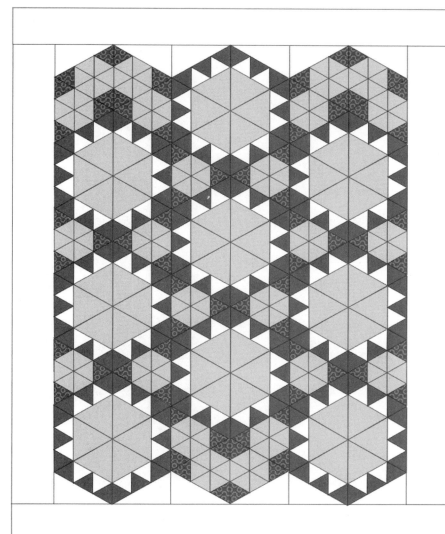

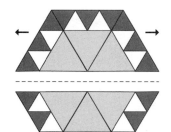

PIECING DIAGRAM
Press seams away from center
Pinch and pin center

TRIM

1. Cut for one block:

1.	6	center*	6¼"	triangle
2.	6	light	3½"	triangle
3.	12	dark	3¼"	diamond

Directions:

2. Using a center* triangle, one light 3½" triangle, and two 3¼" diamonds, assemble one wedge as shown. Make six of these.

3. Sew the wedges three and three and sew across the middle to complete the hexagon block.

All cutting is based on the 3½" triangle size.

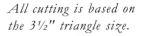

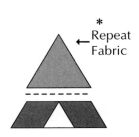

* ← Repeat Fabric

Wedge Piecing Diagram

One Wedge

TRIM BLOCK

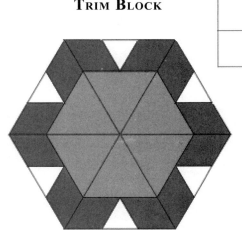

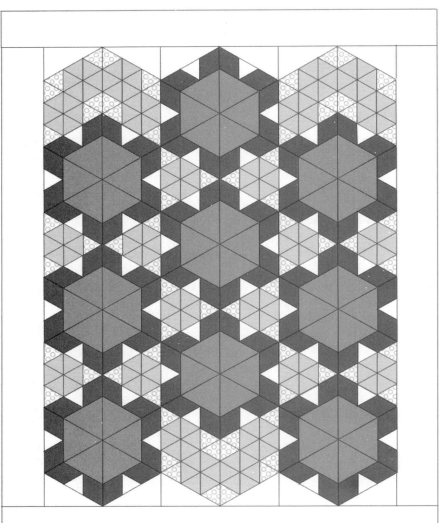

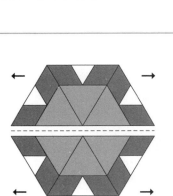

PIECING DIAGRAM
Press seams away
from center
Pinch and pin center

BEANIE

1. Cut for one block::

1.	6	center*	6¼"	triangle
2.	6	light	3½"	triangle
3.	12	dark	4⅞"	flat pyramid (from 3¼" strip)

All cutting is based on the 3½" triangle size.

Directions:

2. Use one center triangle, one light triangle, and two flat pyramids to make one wedge. Make six of these.

3. Sew the wedges together into two sets of three. Pinch and pin and sew all the way across to join the two halves and complete the hexagon block.

Pieced Strip

*
← Repeat Fabric

Wedge Piecing Diagram

One Wedge

BEANIE BLOCK

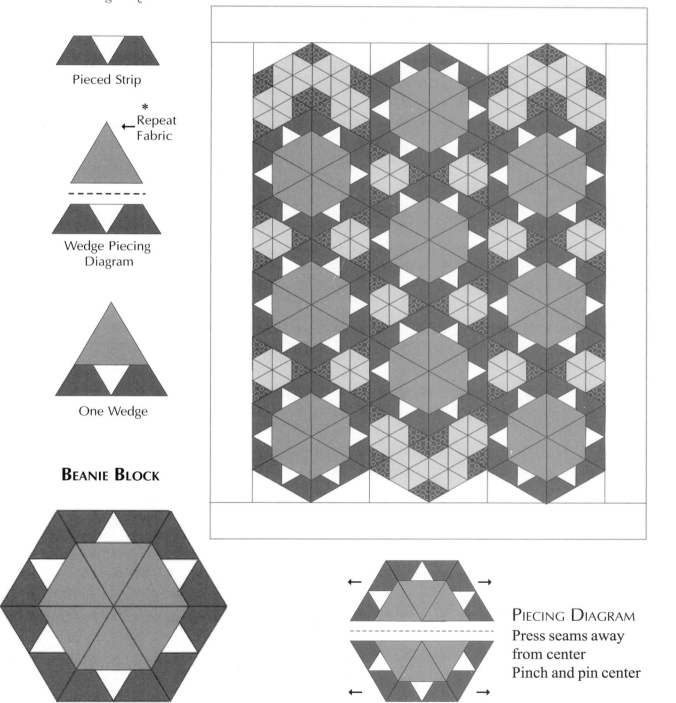

PIECING DIAGRAM
Press seams away from center
Pinch and pin center

Visual Index - Serendipity Quilt Layouts

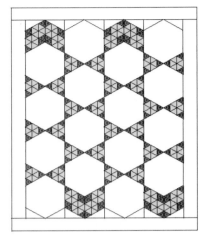

16-Block Quilt, pg. 90

10-Block Quilt, pg. 91

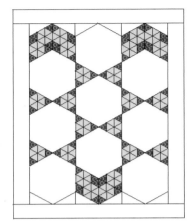

9-Block Quilt, pg. 92

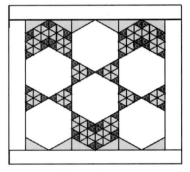

6-Block Quilt, pg. 93

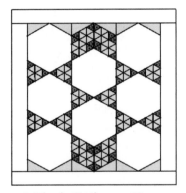

8-Block Quilt, pg. 93

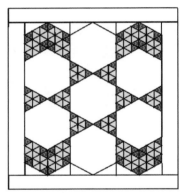

7-Block Quilt, pg. 94

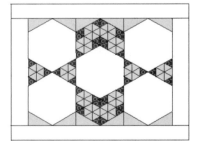

5-Block Quilt, pg. 95

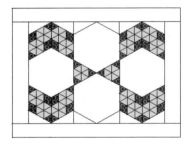

4-Block Quilt, pg. 95

The 10-Block Quilt, the 7-Block Quilt, and the 4-Block Quilt have Triangle Half and Star corners as extra layout possibilities.

1-Block Quilt, pg. 96

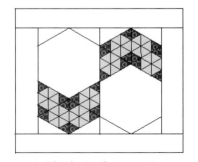

2-Block Quilt, pg. 96

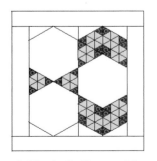

3-Block Quilt, pg. 89

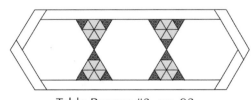

Table Runner #2, pg. 92

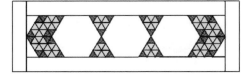

Table Runner #1, pg. 89

PUTTING IT ALL TOGETHER

When I have the first set of stacked repeats laid out in a hexagon or star, I choose the accent and support fabrics to make the other parts of this wedge-based block. An assortment is pulled from my collection, and the first block is made. Then I lay out another stacked repeat hex or star, and choose the next set of support fabrics for another block from my pulled group of fabrics. After a few blocks, and looking at what I have already made, I may repeat some favorite color combinations until enough blocks have been created. Other quilt artists may plan ahead and choose their fabrics with more thoughtful planning. My approach means I won't run out of fabric, because another fabric can always be added. *Note: In the quilt diagrams on the following pages, yardage is given for the triangles of background fabric, but I usually make the triangles from a combination of fabrics, not just one.*

SETTING TRIANGLES

To construct a Serendipity Setting Triangle, sew six layered pattern repeat (center*) triangles into two sets of three, pin to match centers and sew across the middle. Sew three background fabric 3½" triangles onto three separate sides of the resulting pieced hexagon.

Pieced Hexagon

The basic setting triangle is made from:

6	center*	3½"	triangles
3	accent	3½"	triangles

Serendipity Setting Triangle

SUBSTITUTIONS & VARIATIONS

To add another design element to the quilt, or if you run out of pattern repeats, try substituting these hexagons in the setting triangles:

1. A hexagon made from 3½" triangles of two different fabrics sewed alternately.

Six 3½" Triangles

6" Hexagon

2. A hexagon cut from a 6" strip. (Cut a 6" diamond, then cut a 3" trangle from each end.) Find a pretty motif and center the hexagon on this.

1⅞" Diamonds & 2⅛" Triangles

3. A little star made from 1⅞" diamonds and 2⅛" triangles. Sew two triangles to a diamond. Press to the triangles. Make six of these pieced triangles. Sew three and three. Press out from the center. Pinch and pin the center. Sew across the middle.

4. A little star made from 2⅛" triangles. Assemble six wedges. Sew three and three, pressing out. Pinch, pin, and sew as in #3.

Whatever you put in place of the stacked repeat hexagon, sew three 3½" triangles (light, medium, or dark fabric as you choose) on three separate sides to make a Serendipity Setting Triangle.

Or even more variety: substitute a solid 9" triangle or three diamonds and three triangles to make a different setting triangle.

Pieced With 2⅛" Triangles

Plain 9" Triangle

Pieced 9" Triangle

FINISH THE QUILT TOP

Sew blocks and setting triangles into vertical rows as shown in the quilt diagram you choose. Different quilt layouts require different numbers of blocks and setting triangles. Rows (often) alternately begin with a block at the top and four setting triangles to finish the bottom, or the other way around. Square off both ends of each row with triangle halves cut from a 5½" x 9½" rectangle.

OR: Square off both ends of each row with a Fill-In Piece constructed from a 4⅞" triangle plus a 2⅞" diamond half . Sew the rows together as shown in the quilt diagram. Complete with borders as desired.

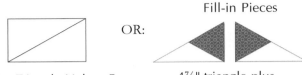

FINISH TOP AND BOTTOM OF ROWS

Fill-in Pieces

OR:

Cut Triangle Halves From a 5½" x 9½" Rectangle

4⅞" triangle plus 2⅞" diamond half

| 3½" triangle | **3-Block Table Runner #1** | Without Borders: 17" x 77" |

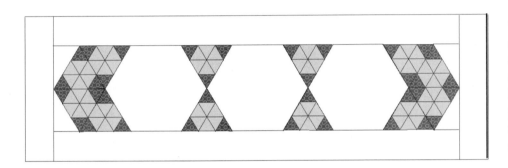

This 3-Block Table Runner is easy to put together as a fancy touch for a special dinner. You may use leftover blocks to make this easy project. Make a shorter table runner by leaving off the setting triangles at each end.

3½" triangle
3-Block Quilt
Without Borders: 33½" x 38¾"

10 Setting Triangles:
(30 background 3½" triangles)
7" accent fabric for setting triangles
5½" fabric for fill-in pieces

The 3-Block Quilt is assembled in two vertical rows, with one row having two blocks and two setting triangles, and the second row having one block and eight setting triangles. With borders, it is exactly baby quilt size. Extra blocks can make this great little quilt.

Piecing Diagram

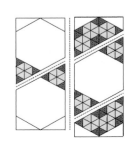

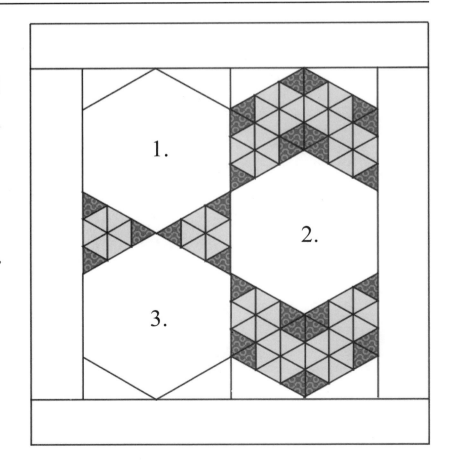

All fabrics 42" wide prewashed.

Fabric Requirements: these are suggestions and estimates.

First – Up to four high contrast large print fabrics – each with six repeats

40 Setting Triangles: (120 background 3½" triangles)
1 yd. fabric for 3½" background triangles
½ yd. fabric for fill-in pieces at top and bottom

IF stacked repeat shape in block is:

3½" triangle	Minimum Needed	2 yd. fabric
3¼" diamond		2¼ yd.
4⅞" triangle		2½ yd.
4⅝" diamond		3¼ yd.
6¼" triangle		3½ yd.

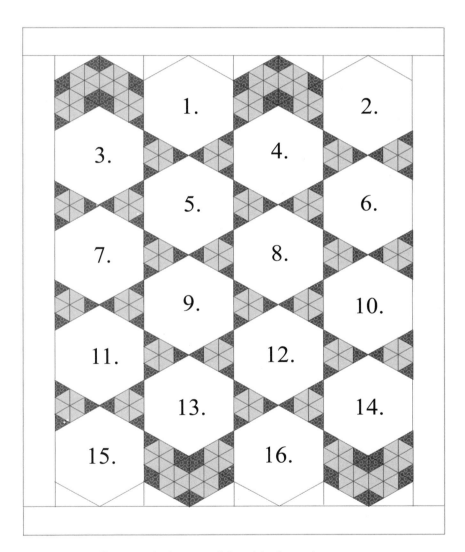

Piecing Diagram

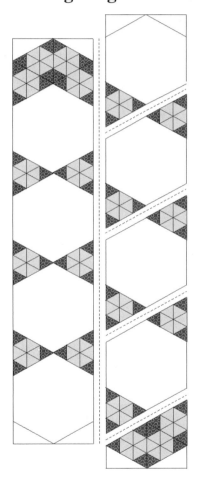

Piece the quilt in vertical rows of four blocks each. Each block begins with a block and ends with four setting triangles as shown. The second and fourth row are turned upside down. Lay out the blocks and setting triangles on a floor or wall for the best arrangement before beginning to sew the blocks into rows. Then sew the rows together to make the quilt top. Add borders as desired.

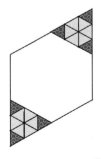

Basic Units

10-Block Quilt
Without Borders: 50" x 77"

All fabrics 42" wide prewashed.
Fabric Requirements:
These are suggestions and estimates.
30 Setting Triangles:
(90 background 3½" triangles)
1 yd. fabric for setting triangles
⅓" yd. fabric for fill-in pieces

No piecing diagram is given. The quilt is pieced in three rows. The center row consists of four blocks and six setting triangles. The two ouside rows each have three blocks and 12 setting triangles. Or, make three rows as in the variation below right, squaring off the elongated hexagon with left and right triangle halves cut from a 16" x 27½" rectangle. (Place two rectangles right or wrong sides together and cut corner-to-corner.) If you use the triangle half corners, or the star corners, fabric requirements will be different.

16" x 27½" Rectangle Bisected

See pg. 94 for more instructions on how to put together the Star Corner, including a piecing diagram. Choices of fabric, judging color, pattern, texture and value add to or subtract from the effectiveness of any design or layout. But it's fun to learn!

With Star Corners

With Triangle Half Corners

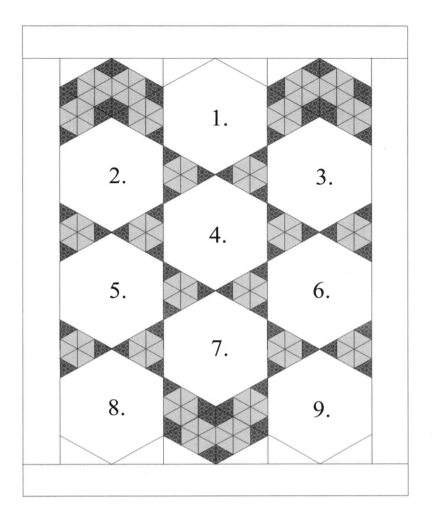

All fabrics 42" wide prewashed.
Fabric Requirements: these are suggestions and estimates.
One high contrast large print fabric – six repeats
24 Setting Triangles: (72 background 3½" triangles)
½ yd. fabric background triangles
⅓ yd. fabric for fill-in pieces at top and bottom

The 9-Block Quilt is assembled in three identical vertical rows, with the center row turned upside down. With borders, it makes a twin-sized quilt. It's big enough to have fun with, giving lots of variety in the block designs and setting triangles, while small enough not to become a chore. As a diagram, it shows enough blocks to demonstrate secondary designs created in a quilt layout, and so the author used it on each page of the block designs.

Piecing Diagram

3½" triangle   **3-Block Table Runner #2**   Without Borders: 17" x 57½"

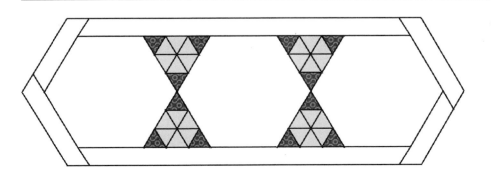

This smaller Table Runner is quick to make, with only the three blocks and four setting triangles in all. A narrow outside border finishes it off as an elongated hexagon. Or, square it off, like the table runner on pg. 89.

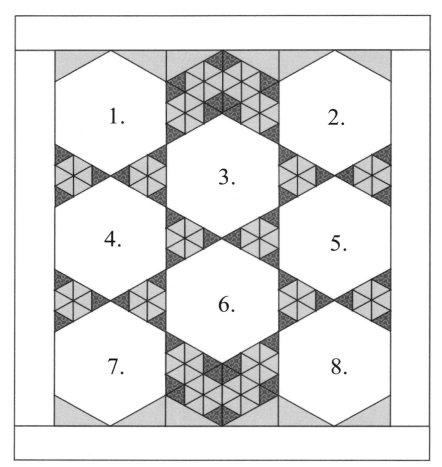

8-Block Quilt

Without Borders: 50" x 58"

The 8-Block Quilt is assembled in three vertical rows, with three blocks and four setting triangles in the outside rows, and two blocks and 10 setting triangles in the center row. Fill-in pieces are added to each row as shown, before the rows are sewn together. With borders, it makes a twin sized quilt. Another very populay layout.

All fabrics 42" wide prewashed.
Fabric Requirements:
suggestions and estimates
18 Setting Triangles:
(54 background 3½" triangles)
½ yd. fabric for setting triangles
⅓ yd. fabric for fill-in pieces

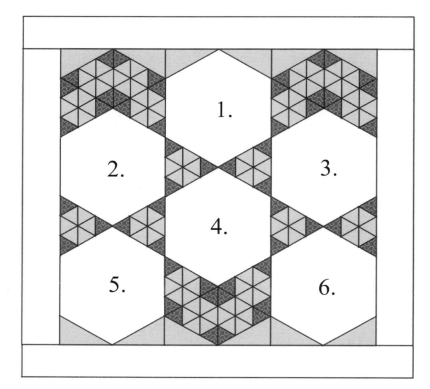

3½" triangle
6-Block Quilt

Without Borders: 50" x 48½"

The 6-Block Quilt is assembled in three vertical rows, with two blocks and six setting triangles in each row. The center row is assembled upside down. Fill-in pieces are added to each row as shown, before the rows are sewn together. With borders, it makes a wall hanging or throw.

All fabrics 42" wide prewashed.
Fabric Requirements:
suggestions and estimates
18 Setting Triangles:
(54 background 3½" triangles)
½ yd. fabric for setting triangles
⅓ yd. fabric for fill-in pieces

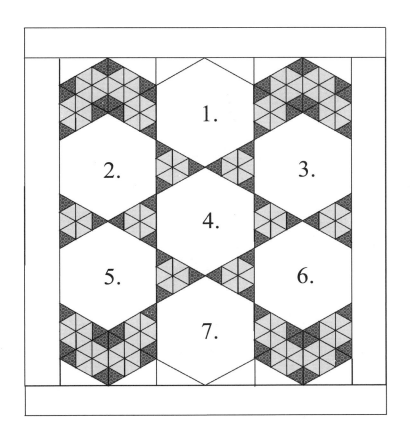

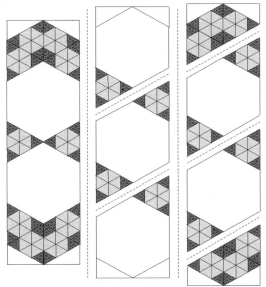

Piecing Diagram

An alternate version of the 7-block quilt squares off the hexagon with left and right triangle halves from a 16" x 27½" rectangle. (See pg. 90. Or cut a larger than 26" triangle, cut it in half down the center, and trim to square up after the triangle halves are sewn on.) The 4-Block quilt can also use these large triangle halves for less work and a faster finish. Or put stars in the corners of your quilt for a different look.

All fabrics 42" wide prewashed.
Fabric Requirements:
suggestions and estimates
24 Setting Triangles:
(72 background 3½" triangles)
¾ yd. fabric for setting triangles
⅓" yd. fabric for fill-in pieces

Star Corners

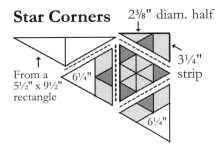

2⅜" diam. half

3¼" strip

From a 5½" x 9½" rectangle

6¼"

6¼"

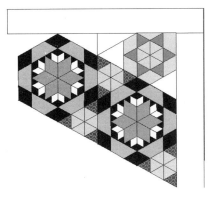

You can float a star in the corners of your 10-Block, 7-Block or 4-Block quilt. The large background triangles are 6¼" and the other pieces need-ed are fill-in pieces: 3¼" diamonds, 3½" triangles, a 3¼" strip trimmed to a 60° angle, and a diamond half cut from a 2⅞" strip.

With Triangle Half Corners

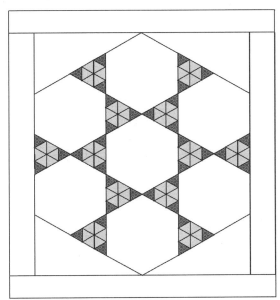

3½" triangle
5-Block Quilt
Without Borders: 33½" x 50"

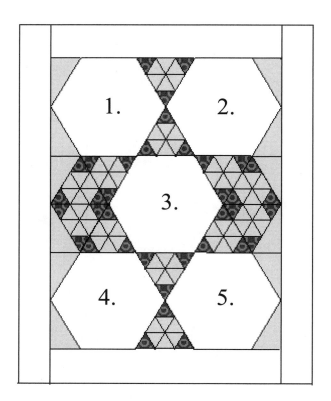

The 5-Block Quilt is assembled in three horizontal rows, with two blocks and two setting triangles in the top and bottom row, and one block and eight setting triangles in the center row. Fill-in pieces are added to each row as shown, before the rows are sewn together. With borders, it makes a wall hanging or child's quilt.

All fabrics 42" wide prewashed.
Fabric Requirements: suggestions and estimates
12 Setting Triangles: (36 background 3½" triangles)
⅓ yd. background fabric for setting triangles
5½" fabric for fill-in pieces

3½" triangle
4-Block Quilt
Without Borders: 50" x 33½"

10 Setting Triangles:
(30 background 3½" triangles)
7" fabric for setting triangles
5½" fabric for fill-in pieces

Piecing Diagram

The 4-Block Quilt is assembled in three vertical rows, with the center row having two blocks and two setting triangles, and the two end rows having one block and eight setting triangles each as shown. With borders, it is a good size wall hanging. A fast variation uses only six setting triangles, squaring off the resulting diamond shape with left and right triangle halves cut from 16" x 27½" rectangles. (See pg. 90.)

With Triangle Half Corners

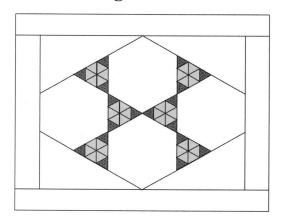

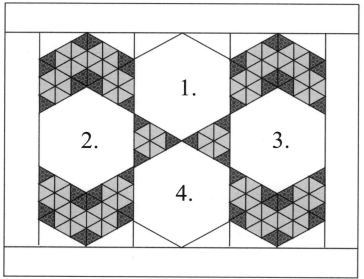

All fabrics 42" wide prewashed.
Fabric Requirements: suggestions and estimates
8 Setting Triangles: (24 background 3½" triangles)
7" strip of fabric for setting triangles
5½" fabric for fill-in pieces

The 2-Block Quilt is assembled in two identical vertical rows, with one row turned upside down. With borders, it makes a small wall hanging. Leftover blocks and setting triangles make a gift quilt, or a small quilt can become an experiment in pattern and color.

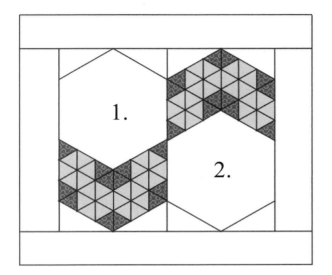

Piecing Diagram

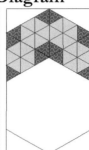

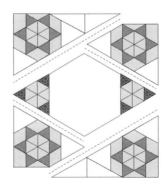

Piecing Diagrams

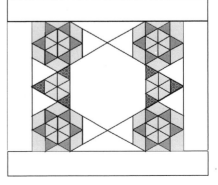

The 1-Block Quilt is assembled with a diamond in the center and four identical sets of three setting triangles each, with fill-in pieces added as shown. With borders, it makes a small wall hanging. One leftover block with setting triangles or their substitutes, can be an art project or a great gift. Try substituting Star Corners for the twelve setting triangles.

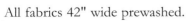

All fabrics 42" wide prewashed.
Fabric Requirements: suggestions and estimates
14 Setting Triangles: (42 background 3½" triangles)
⅓ yd. fabric for setting triangles
5½" fabric for fill-in pieces

Quilt Diagrams To Color - In Alphabetical Order

Some of the quilters testing these patterns requested a White Quilt page to color, since the quilts can be approached and completed in many different ways/looks, depending on the high contrast large print you choose. This addition to the book is the result. Three quilts are given full page size. The other designs are four to a page. Scan and print the page or copy it on a copy machine. Then cut out one quilt design and enlarge it to a full page. OR: Go to www.clearviewtriangle.com and find all 50 full page diagrams to download and print for free.

Quilt Diagrams To Color

BIGTOOTH pg. 24

QUILT DIAGRAMS TO COLOR

THIMBLE STAR pg. 18

QUILT DIAGRAMS TO COLOR

PRICKLY PEAR pg. 28

QUILT DIAGRAMS TO COLOR

BALANCE pg. 67

BEANIE pg. 85

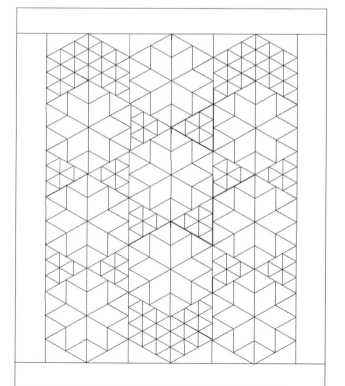

BIG STAR pg. 81

BIG TRIANGLE pg. 19

QUILT DIAGRAMS TO COLOR

BLOOMING pg. 68

BOTANICAL pg. 40

BRILLIANT SKY pg. 37

BUDDING pg. 71

QUILT DIAGRAMS TO COLOR

CACTUS FLOWER pg. 30

CANDLE pg. 34

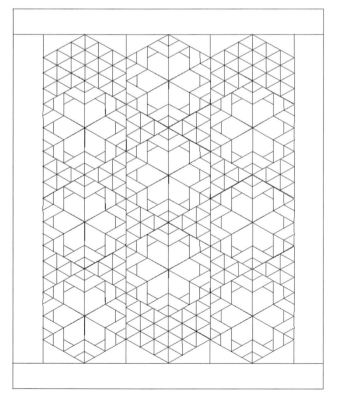

DANCING LOTUS pg. 79

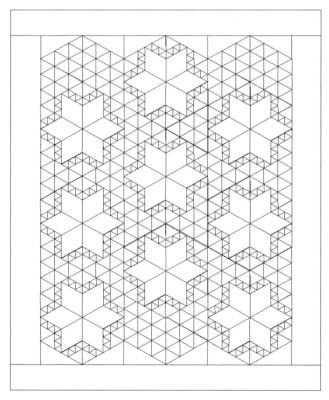

DARK FEATHER pg. 76

QUILT DIAGRAMS TO COLOR

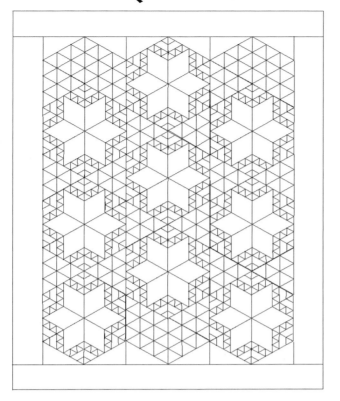

ECHO FEATHER pg. 77

EXPANDING STAR   pg. 46

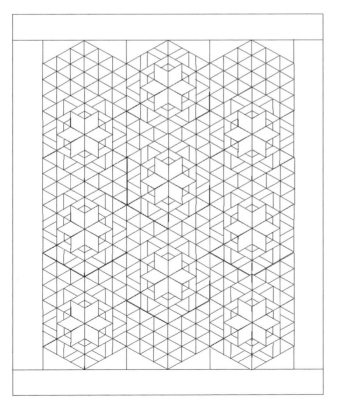

EXPANDING STAR VARIATION pg. 47

FERN pg. 39

QUILT DIAGRAMS TO COLOR

FEATHER pg. 36

FIN pg. 80

FISH pg. 72

FROZEN ROSES pg. 35

Quilt Diagrams To Color

GULL pg. 73

HEARTS pg. 74

ICE CRYSTAL pg. 38

LOG PETAL pg. 26

QUILT DIAGRAMS TO COLOR

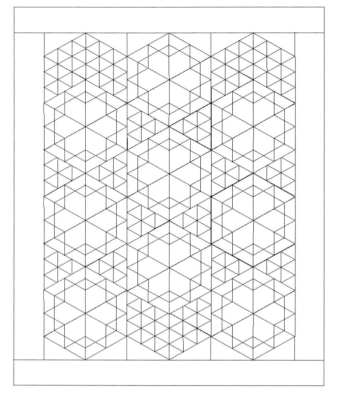

LOTUS FLOWER pg. 78

MARINER'S DELIGHT pg. 22

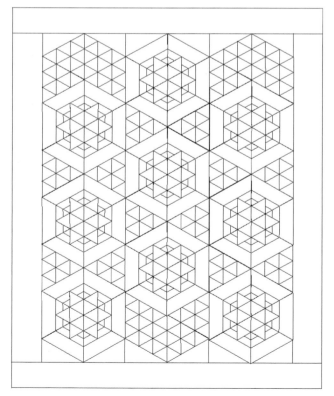

MOONSCAPE pg. 33

NESTED HEARTS pg. 43

QUILT DIAGRAMS TO COLOR

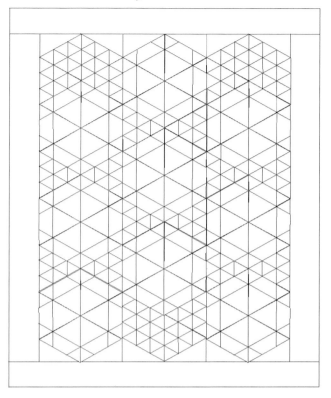

PETAL pg. 82

PINWHEEL pg. 69

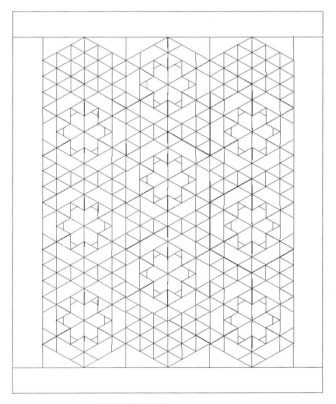

POPCORN pg. 44

RIBBON pg. 66

Quilt Diagrams To Color

ROSE PINWHEEL pg. 70

SEASHELLS pg. 17

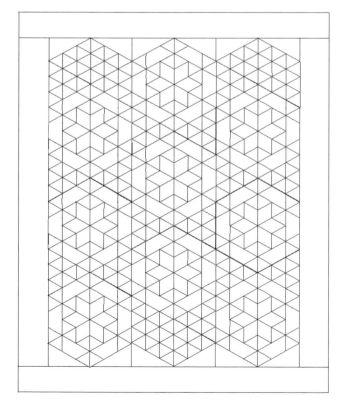

SHERIFF'S STAR pg. 48

SILK STOCKING pg. 41

QUILT DIAGRAMS TO COLOR

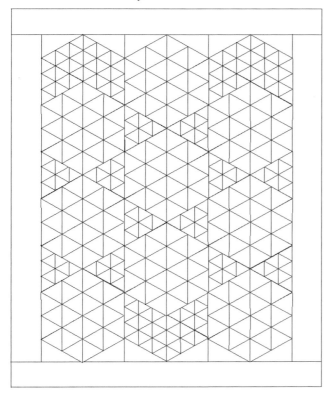

SIMPLE CROCHET pg. 75

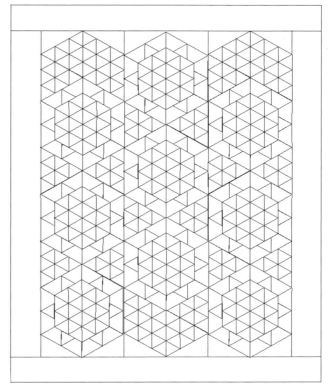

SNOWFALL pg. 23

SPARKLING SKY pg. 65

SUNRISE pg. 32

QUILT DIAGRAMS TO COLOR

TEXAS SUNFLOWER pg. 16

TOOTH pg. 83

TORCH pg. 42

TRIM pg. 84

Quilt Diagrams To Color

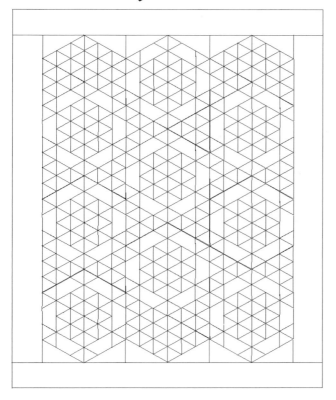

WATERCRYSTAL pg. 27

WEDGE CIRCLE pg. 20

WEDGE STAR pg. 21

WINGS OF A DOVE pg. 45

Special Thanks To These Manufacturers:

Alexander Henry Textiles

Andover Fabrics/Makower uk

The Ehrlanger Group/Woodrow Studios

Free Spirit Fabric

Hoffman California International Fabrics

In The Beginning Fabric

Kona Bay Fabrics

Michael Miller Fabrics, Inc.

P&B Textiles

Robert Kaufman Co.

Kelsul, Inc. Quilter's "Dream" Cotton™ Batting

To learn more about stacked pattern repeats, read Bethany Reynolds' books, "Magic Stack 'N Whack Quilts®", "Stack 'N Whackier," and "Magic Quilts-By The Slice ."

Contact Bethany Reynolds:
B&R Design, Inc.
P.O. Box 1374
Ellsworth, ME 04605
Website: http://www.quilt.com/BReynolds

OTHER PRODUCTS FROM CLEARVIEW TRIANGLE

60° Triangle Books and Tools

B-25	19.95	Book - Big Book Of Building Block Quilts
B-21	14.95	Book - Sensational 6-Pointed Star Quilts
SR-20	16.95	Super 60 (Combination Triangle Tool)
DG-27	6.75	Diamond Guide (Super 60 Add-On)
MP-3	11.50	8" Mini-Pro
CT-1	8.00	6" triangle
CT-2	15.00	12" triangle
GP-12	5.95	2-sided Graph Paper-Pad of 30 sheets
M-15	11.50	Metric Triangle
M-23	16.95	Metric Super 60

Quick Picture Quilts - Blocks Based On Squares

QA-28 $17.95   Book - Quilted Adventures

Bargain Corner

ZO 18	$15.00	Book - Patchwork Zoo
EA –7	5.00	Book - Easy & Elegant Quilts
MA-14	5.00	Book - Mock Appliqué
HH-17	4.00	Book - Happy Halloween
TX-23	4.00	Book - Special Times
TC-24	4.00	Book - Town & Country
MC-16	4.00	Book - Merry Christmas
NL-19	3.00	Book - New Labels
PR-22	3.00	Pattern - Pigma® Pen Roll-Up

Order From:

CLEARVIEW TRIANGLE
8311 - 180th St S. E.
Snohomish, WA 98296
Tel: 1-360-668-4151
Fax: 1-360-668-6338
Orders: 1-888-901-4151

Shipping Charges:

Order Amount	Shipping
0.00 - 5.99	1.99
6.00 - 10.99	2.99
11.00 - 20.99	3.99
21.00 - 30.99	4.99
31.00 - 40.99	5.99
41.00 - 65.99	6.99
66.00 - 100.99	7.99
101.00+	9.00

International customers may have additional shipping costs.
Wash. residents add 8.9% sales tax.
Tools usually shipped UPS, Books U.S. Mail.
We take Visa and Mastercard.

E-mail: sara@clearviewtriangle.com
Website:www.clearviewtriangle.com